C-4803 CAREER EXAMINATION SERIES

This is your
PASSBOOK for...

Electrical Mechanic

Test Preparation Study Guide
Questions & Answers

COPYRIGHT NOTICE

This book is SOLELY intended for, is sold ONLY to, and its use is RESTRICTED to individual, bona fide applicants or candidates who qualify by virtue of having seriously filed applications for appropriate license, certificate, professional and/or promotional advancement, higher school matriculation, scholarship, or other legitimate requirements of education and/or governmental authorities.

This book is NOT intended for use, class instruction, tutoring, training, duplication, copying, reprinting, excerption, or adaptation, etc., by:

1) Other publishers
2) Proprietors and/or Instructors of "Coaching" and/or Preparatory Courses
3) Personnel and/or Training Divisions of commercial, industrial, and governmental organizations
4) Schools, colleges, or universities and/or their departments and staffs, including teachers and other personnel
5) Testing Agencies or Bureaus
6) Study groups which seek by the purchase of a single volume to copy and/or duplicate and/or adapt this material for use by the group as a whole without having purchased individual volumes for each of the members of the group
7) Et al.

Such persons would be in violation of appropriate Federal and State statutes.

PROVISION OF LICENSING AGREEMENTS – Recognized educational, commercial, industrial, and governmental institutions and organizations, and others legitimately engaged in educational pursuits, including training, testing, and measurement activities, may address request for a licensing agreement to the copyright owners, who will determine whether, and under what conditions, including fees and charges, the materials in this book may be used them. In other words, a licensing facility exists for the legitimate use of the material in this book on other than an individual basis. However, it is asseverated and affirmed here that the material in this book CANNOT be used without the receipt of the express permission of such a licensing agreement from the Publishers. Inquiries re licensing should be addressed to the company, attention rights and permissions department.

All rights reserved, including the right of reproduction in whole or in part, in any form or by any means, electronic or mechanical, including photocopying, recording, or by any information storage and retrieval system, without permission in writing from the Publisher.

Copyright © 2024 by
National Learning Corporation

212 Michael Drive, Syosset, NY 11791
(516) 921-8888 • www.passbooks.com
E-mail: info@passbooks.com

PUBLISHED IN THE UNITED STATES OF AMERICA

PASSBOOK® SERIES

THE *PASSBOOK® SERIES* has been created to prepare applicants and candidates for the ultimate academic battlefield – the examination room.

At some time in our lives, each and every one of us may be required to take an examination – for validation, matriculation, admission, qualification, registration, certification, or licensure.

Based on the assumption that every applicant or candidate has met the basic formal educational standards, has taken the required number of courses, and read the necessary texts, the *PASSBOOK® SERIES* furnishes the one special preparation which may assure passing with confidence, instead of failing with insecurity. Examination questions – together with answers – are furnished as the basic vehicle for study so that the mysteries of the examination and its compounding difficulties may be eliminated or diminished by a sure method.

This book is meant to help you pass your examination provided that you qualify and are serious in your objective.

The entire field is reviewed through the huge store of content information which is succinctly presented through a provocative and challenging approach – the question-and-answer method.

A climate of success is established by furnishing the correct answers at the end of each test.

You soon learn to recognize types of questions, forms of questions, and patterns of questioning. You may even begin to anticipate expected outcomes.

You perceive that many questions are repeated or adapted so that you can gain acute insights, which may enable you to score many sure points.

You learn how to confront new questions, or types of questions, and to attack them confidently and work out the correct answers.

You note objectives and emphases, and recognize pitfalls and dangers, so that you may make positive educational adjustments.

Moreover, you are kept fully informed in relation to new concepts, methods, practices, and directions in the field.

You discover that you are actually taking the examination all the time: you are preparing for the examination by "taking" an examination, not by reading extraneous and/or supererogatory textbooks.

In short, this PASSBOOK®, used directedly, should be an important factor in helping you to pass your test.

ELECTRICAL MECHANIC

DUTIES:
An Electrical Mechanic performs skilled mechanical and electrical work in the installation and maintenance of high and low voltage electrical circuits and related equipment at electrical stations and plants such as electrical substations; receiving, distributing, and customer stations; steam generating stations; water pumping and chlorinating stations; converter stations; hydro-electric plants; high voltage switching stations; and similar facilities and buildings; and performs other related duties.

THE SCOPE OF THE EXAMINATION:
The examination will consist of a qualifying written test and performance test. In the qualifying written test, which will consist of multiple-choice questions, candidates may be examined for knowledge of scales and units of measurement used in electric stations; hand and power tools; arithmetic and algebra; the ability to read scales, dials, and digital readouts; visualize effects of forces upon a given load (mechanical comprehension); using street maps; oral/written communication; and other necessary skills, knowledge, and abilities.

HOW TO TAKE A TEST

I. YOU MUST PASS AN EXAMINATION

A. *WHAT EVERY CANDIDATE SHOULD KNOW*

Examination applicants often ask us for help in preparing for the written test. What can I study in advance? What kinds of questions will be asked? How will the test be given? How will the papers be graded?

As an applicant for a civil service examination, you may be wondering about some of these things. Our purpose here is to suggest effective methods of advance study and to describe civil service examinations.

Your chances for success on this examination can be increased if you know how to prepare. Those "pre-examination jitters" can be reduced if you know what to expect. You can even experience an adventure in good citizenship if you know why civil service exams are given.

B. *WHY ARE CIVIL SERVICE EXAMINATIONS GIVEN?*

Civil service examinations are important to you in two ways. As a citizen, you want public jobs filled by employees who know how to do their work. As a job seeker, you want a fair chance to compete for that job on an equal footing with other candidates. The best-known means of accomplishing this two-fold goal is the competitive examination.

Exams are widely publicized throughout the nation. They may be administered for jobs in federal, state, city, municipal, town or village governments or agencies.

Any citizen may apply, with some limitations, such as the age or residence of applicants. Your experience and education may be reviewed to see whether you meet the requirements for the particular examination. When these requirements exist, they are reasonable and applied consistently to all applicants. Thus, a competitive examination may cause you some uneasiness now, but it is your privilege and safeguard.

C. *HOW ARE CIVIL SERVICE EXAMS DEVELOPED?*

Examinations are carefully written by trained technicians who are specialists in the field known as "psychological measurement," in consultation with recognized authorities in the field of work that the test will cover. These experts recommend the subject matter areas or skills to be tested; only those knowledges or skills important to your success on the job are included. The most reliable books and source materials available are used as references. Together, the experts and technicians judge the difficulty level of the questions.

Test technicians know how to phrase questions so that the problem is clearly stated. Their ethics do not permit "trick" or "catch" questions. Questions may have been tried out on sample groups, or subjected to statistical analysis, to determine their usefulness.

Written tests are often used in combination with performance tests, ratings of training and experience, and oral interviews. All of these measures combine to form the best-known means of finding the right person for the right job.

II. HOW TO PASS THE WRITTEN TEST

A. NATURE OF THE EXAMINATION

To prepare intelligently for civil service examinations, you should know how they differ from school examinations you have taken. In school you were assigned certain definite pages to read or subjects to cover. The examination questions were quite detailed and usually emphasized memory. Civil service exams, on the other hand, try to discover your present ability to perform the duties of a position, plus your potentiality to learn these duties. In other words, a civil service exam attempts to predict how successful you will be. Questions cover such a broad area that they cannot be as minute and detailed as school exam questions.

In the public service similar kinds of work, or positions, are grouped together in one "class." This process is known as *position-classification*. All the positions in a class are paid according to the salary range for that class. One class title covers all of these positions, and they are all tested by the same examination.

B. FOUR BASIC STEPS

1) Study the announcement

How, then, can you know what subjects to study? Our best answer is: "Learn as much as possible about the class of positions for which you've applied." The exam will test the knowledge, skills and abilities needed to do the work.

Your most valuable source of information about the position you want is the official exam announcement. This announcement lists the training and experience qualifications. Check these standards and apply only if you come reasonably close to meeting them.

The brief description of the position in the examination announcement offers some clues to the subjects which will be tested. Think about the job itself. Review the duties in your mind. Can you perform them, or are there some in which you are rusty? Fill in the blank spots in your preparation.

Many jurisdictions preview the written test in the exam announcement by including a section called "Knowledge and Abilities Required," "Scope of the Examination," or some similar heading. Here you will find out specifically what fields will be tested.

2) Review your own background

Once you learn in general what the position is all about, and what you need to know to do the work, ask yourself which subjects you already know fairly well and which need improvement. You may wonder whether to concentrate on improving your strong areas or on building some background in your fields of weakness. When the announcement has specified "some knowledge" or "considerable knowledge," or has used adjectives like "beginning principles of…" or "advanced … methods," you can get a clue as to the number and difficulty of questions to be asked in any given field. More questions, and hence broader coverage, would be included for those subjects which are more important in the work. Now weigh your strengths and weaknesses against the job requirements and prepare accordingly.

3) Determine the level of the position

Another way to tell how intensively you should prepare is to understand the level of the job for which you are applying. Is it the entering level? In other words, is this the position in which beginners in a field of work are hired? Or is it an intermediate or advanced level? Sometimes this is indicated by such words as "Junior" or "Senior" in the class title. Other jurisdictions use Roman numerals to designate the level – Clerk I, Clerk II, for example. The word "Supervisor" sometimes appears in the title. If the level is not indicated by the title, check the description of duties. Will you be working under very close supervision, or will you have responsibility for independent decisions in this work?

4) Choose appropriate study materials

Now that you know the subjects to be examined and the relative amount of each subject to be covered, you can choose suitable study materials. For beginning level jobs, or even advanced ones, if you have a pronounced weakness in some aspect of your training, read a modern, standard textbook in that field. Be sure it is up to date and has general coverage. Such books are normally available at your library, and the librarian will be glad to help you locate one. For entry-level positions, questions of appropriate difficulty are chosen – neither highly advanced questions, nor those too simple. Such questions require careful thought but not advanced training.

If the position for which you are applying is technical or advanced, you will read more advanced, specialized material. If you are already familiar with the basic principles of your field, elementary textbooks would waste your time. Concentrate on advanced textbooks and technical periodicals. Think through the concepts and review difficult problems in your field.

These are all general sources. You can get more ideas on your own initiative, following these leads. For example, training manuals and publications of the government agency which employs workers in your field can be useful, particularly for technical and professional positions. A letter or visit to the government department involved may result in more specific study suggestions, and certainly will provide you with a more definite idea of the exact nature of the position you are seeking.

III. KINDS OF TESTS

Tests are used for purposes other than measuring knowledge and ability to perform specified duties. For some positions, it is equally important to test ability to make adjustments to new situations or to profit from training. In others, basic mental abilities not dependent on information are essential. Questions which test these things may not appear as pertinent to the duties of the position as those which test for knowledge and information. Yet they are often highly important parts of a fair examination. For very general questions, it is almost impossible to help you direct your study efforts. What we can do is to point out some of the more common of these general abilities needed in public service positions and describe some typical questions.

1) General information

Broad, general information has been found useful for predicting job success in some kinds of work. This is tested in a variety of ways, from vocabulary lists to questions about current events. Basic background in some field of work, such as sociology or economics, may be sampled in a group of questions. Often these are principles which have become familiar to most persons through exposure rather than through formal training. It is difficult to advise you how to study for these questions; being alert to the world around you is our best suggestion.

2) Verbal ability

An example of an ability needed in many positions is verbal or language ability. Verbal ability is, in brief, the ability to use and understand words. Vocabulary and grammar tests are typical measures of this ability. Reading comprehension or paragraph interpretation questions are common in many kinds of civil service tests. You are given a paragraph of written material and asked to find its central meaning.

3) Numerical ability
Number skills can be tested by the familiar arithmetic problem, by checking paired lists of numbers to see which are alike and which are different, or by interpreting charts and graphs. In the latter test, a graph may be printed in the test booklet which you are asked to use as the basis for answering questions.

4) Observation
A popular test for law-enforcement positions is the observation test. A picture is shown to you for several minutes, then taken away. Questions about the picture test your ability to observe both details and larger elements.

5) Following directions
In many positions in the public service, the employee must be able to carry out written instructions dependably and accurately. You may be given a chart with several columns, each column listing a variety of information. The questions require you to carry out directions involving the information given in the chart.

6) Skills and aptitudes
Performance tests effectively measure some manual skills and aptitudes. When the skill is one in which you are trained, such as typing or shorthand, you can practice. These tests are often very much like those given in business school or high school courses. For many of the other skills and aptitudes, however, no short-time preparation can be made. Skills and abilities natural to you or that you have developed throughout your lifetime are being tested.

Many of the general questions just described provide all the data needed to answer the questions and ask you to use your reasoning ability to find the answers. Your best preparation for these tests, as well as for tests of facts and ideas, is to be at your physical and mental best. You, no doubt, have your own methods of getting into an exam-taking mood and keeping "in shape." The next section lists some ideas on this subject.

IV. KINDS OF QUESTIONS

Only rarely is the "essay" question, which you answer in narrative form, used in civil service tests. Civil service tests are usually of the short-answer type. Full instructions for answering these questions will be given to you at the examination. But in case this is your first experience with short-answer questions and separate answer sheets, here is what you need to know:

1) Multiple-choice Questions
Most popular of the short-answer questions is the "multiple choice" or "best answer" question. It can be used, for example, to test for factual knowledge, ability to solve problems or judgment in meeting situations found at work.

A multiple-choice question is normally one of three types—
- It can begin with an incomplete statement followed by several possible endings. You are to find the one ending which *best* completes the statement, although some of the others may not be entirely wrong.
- It can also be a complete statement in the form of a question which is answered by choosing one of the statements listed.

- It can be in the form of a problem – again you select the best answer.

Here is an example of a multiple-choice question with a discussion which should give you some clues as to the method for choosing the right answer:

When an employee has a complaint about his assignment, the action which will *best* help him overcome his difficulty is to
- A. discuss his difficulty with his coworkers
- B. take the problem to the head of the organization
- C. take the problem to the person who gave him the assignment
- D. say nothing to anyone about his complaint

In answering this question, you should study each of the choices to find which is best. Consider choice "A" – Certainly an employee may discuss his complaint with fellow employees, but no change or improvement can result, and the complaint remains unresolved. Choice "B" is a poor choice since the head of the organization probably does not know what assignment you have been given, and taking your problem to him is known as "going over the head" of the supervisor. The supervisor, or person who made the assignment, is the person who can clarify it or correct any injustice. Choice "C" is, therefore, correct. To say nothing, as in choice "D," is unwise. Supervisors have and interest in knowing the problems employees are facing, and the employee is seeking a solution to his problem.

2) True/False Questions

The "true/false" or "right/wrong" form of question is sometimes used. Here a complete statement is given. Your job is to decide whether the statement is right or wrong.

SAMPLE: A roaming cell-phone call to a nearby city costs less than a non-roaming call to a distant city.

This statement is wrong, or false, since roaming calls are more expensive.

This is not a complete list of all possible question forms, although most of the others are variations of these common types. You will always get complete directions for answering questions. Be sure you understand *how* to mark your answers – ask questions until you do.

V. RECORDING YOUR ANSWERS

Computer terminals are used more and more today for many different kinds of exams.
For an examination with very few applicants, you may be told to record your answers in the test booklet itself. Separate answer sheets are much more common. If this separate answer sheet is to be scored by machine – and this is often the case – it is highly important that you mark your answers correctly in order to get credit.
An electronic scoring machine is often used in civil service offices because of the speed with which papers can be scored. Machine-scored answer sheets must be marked with a pencil, which will be given to you. This pencil has a high graphite content which responds to the electronic scoring machine. As a matter of fact, stray dots may register as answers, so do not let your pencil rest on the answer sheet while you are pondering the correct answer. Also, if your pencil lead breaks or is otherwise defective, ask for another.

Since the answer sheet will be dropped in a slot in the scoring machine, be careful not to bend the corners or get the paper crumpled.

The answer sheet normally has five vertical columns of numbers, with 30 numbers to a column. These numbers correspond to the question numbers in your test booklet. After each number, going across the page are four or five pairs of dotted lines. These short dotted lines have small letters or numbers above them. The first two pairs may also have a "T" or "F" above the letters. This indicates that the first two pairs only are to be used if the questions are of the true-false type. If the questions are multiple choice, disregard the "T" and "F" and pay attention only to the small letters or numbers.

Answer your questions in the manner of the sample that follows:

32. The largest city in the United States is
   A. Washington, D.C.
   B. New York City
   C. Chicago
   D. Detroit
   E. San Francisco

1) Choose the answer you think is best. (New York City is the largest, so "B" is correct.)
2) Find the row of dotted lines numbered the same as the question you are answering. (Find row number 32)
3) Find the pair of dotted lines corresponding to the answer. (Find the pair of lines under the mark "B.")
4) Make a solid black mark between the dotted lines.

VI. BEFORE THE TEST

Common sense will help you find procedures to follow to get ready for an examination. Too many of us, however, overlook these sensible measures. Indeed, nervousness and fatigue have been found to be the most serious reasons why applicants fail to do their best on civil service tests. Here is a list of reminders:

- Begin your preparation early – Don't wait until the last minute to go scurrying around for books and materials or to find out what the position is all about.
- Prepare continuously – An hour a night for a week is better than an all-night cram session. This has been definitely established. What is more, a night a week for a month will return better dividends than crowding your study into a shorter period of time.
- Locate the place of the exam – You have been sent a notice telling you when and where to report for the examination. If the location is in a different town or otherwise unfamiliar to you, it would be well to inquire the best route and learn something about the building.
- Relax the night before the test – Allow your mind to rest. Do not study at all that night. Plan some mild recreation or diversion; then go to bed early and get a good night's sleep.
- Get up early enough to make a leisurely trip to the place for the test – This way unforeseen events, traffic snarls, unfamiliar buildings, etc. will not upset you.
- Dress comfortably – A written test is not a fashion show. You will be known by number and not by name, so wear something comfortable.

- Leave excess paraphernalia at home – Shopping bags and odd bundles will get in your way. You need bring only the items mentioned in the official notice you received; usually everything you need is provided. Do not bring reference books to the exam. They will only confuse those last minutes and be taken away from you when in the test room.
- Arrive somewhat ahead of time – If because of transportation schedules you must get there very early, bring a newspaper or magazine to take your mind off yourself while waiting.
- Locate the examination room – When you have found the proper room, you will be directed to the seat or part of the room where you will sit. Sometimes you are given a sheet of instructions to read while you are waiting. Do not fill out any forms until you are told to do so; just read them and be prepared.
- Relax and prepare to listen to the instructions
- If you have any physical problem that may keep you from doing your best, be sure to tell the test administrator. If you are sick or in poor health, you really cannot do your best on the exam. You can come back and take the test some other time.

VII. AT THE TEST

The day of the test is here and you have the test booklet in your hand. The temptation to get going is very strong. Caution! There is more to success than knowing the right answers. You must know how to identify your papers and understand variations in the type of short-answer question used in this particular examination. Follow these suggestions for maximum results from your efforts:

1) Cooperate with the monitor

The test administrator has a duty to create a situation in which you can be as much at ease as possible. He will give instructions, tell you when to begin, check to see that you are marking your answer sheet correctly, and so on. He is not there to guard you, although he will see that your competitors do not take unfair advantage. He wants to help you do your best.

2) Listen to all instructions

Don't jump the gun! Wait until you understand all directions. In most civil service tests you get more time than you need to answer the questions. So don't be in a hurry. Read each word of instructions until you clearly understand the meaning. Study the examples, listen to all announcements and follow directions. Ask questions if you do not understand what to do.

3) Identify your papers

Civil service exams are usually identified by number only. You will be assigned a number; you must not put your name on your test papers. Be sure to copy your number correctly. Since more than one exam may be given, copy your exact examination title.

4) Plan your time

Unless you are told that a test is a "speed" or "rate of work" test, speed itself is usually not important. Time enough to answer all the questions will be provided, but this does not mean that you have all day. An overall time limit has been set. Divide the total time (in minutes) by the number of questions to determine the approximate time you have for each question.

5) Do not linger over difficult questions

If you come across a difficult question, mark it with a paper clip (useful to have along) and come back to it when you have been through the booklet. One caution if you do this – be sure to skip a number on your answer sheet as well. Check often to be sure that you have not lost your place and that you are marking in the row numbered the same as the question you are answering.

6) Read the questions

Be sure you know what the question asks! Many capable people are unsuccessful because they failed to *read* the questions correctly.

7) Answer all questions

Unless you have been instructed that a penalty will be deducted for incorrect answers, it is better to guess than to omit a question.

8) Speed tests

It is often better NOT to guess on speed tests. It has been found that on timed tests people are tempted to spend the last few seconds before time is called in marking answers at random – without even reading them – in the hope of picking up a few extra points. To discourage this practice, the instructions may warn you that your score will be "corrected" for guessing. That is, a penalty will be applied. The incorrect answers will be deducted from the correct ones, or some other penalty formula will be used.

9) Review your answers

If you finish before time is called, go back to the questions you guessed or omitted to give them further thought. Review other answers if you have time.

10) Return your test materials

If you are ready to leave before others have finished or time is called, take ALL your materials to the monitor and leave quietly. Never take any test material with you. The monitor can discover whose papers are not complete, and taking a test booklet may be grounds for disqualification.

VIII. EXAMINATION TECHNIQUES

1) Read the general instructions carefully. These are usually printed on the first page of the exam booklet. As a rule, these instructions refer to the timing of the examination; the fact that you should not start work until the signal and must stop work at a signal, etc. If there are any *special* instructions, such as a choice of questions to be answered, make sure that you note this instruction carefully.

2) When you are ready to start work on the examination, that is as soon as the signal has been given, read the instructions to each question booklet, underline any key words or phrases, such as *least, best, outline, describe* and the like. In this way you will tend to answer as requested rather than discover on reviewing your paper that you *listed without describing*, that you selected the *worst* choice rather than the *best* choice, etc.

3) If the examination is of the objective or multiple-choice type – that is, each question will also give a series of possible answers: A, B, C or D, and you are called upon to select the best answer and write the letter next to that answer on your answer paper – it is advisable to start answering each question in turn. There may be anywhere from 50 to 100 such questions in the three or four hours allotted and you can see how much time would be taken if you read through all the questions before beginning to answer any. Furthermore, if you come across a question or group of questions which you know would be difficult to answer, it would undoubtedly affect your handling of all the other questions.

4) If the examination is of the essay type and contains but a few questions, it is a moot point as to whether you should read all the questions before starting to answer any one. Of course, if you are given a choice – say five out of seven and the like – then it is essential to read all the questions so you can eliminate the two that are most difficult. If, however, you are asked to answer all the questions, there may be danger in trying to answer the easiest one first because you may find that you will spend too much time on it. The best technique is to answer the first question, then proceed to the second, etc.

5) Time your answers. Before the exam begins, write down the time it started, then add the time allowed for the examination and write down the time it must be completed, then divide the time available somewhat as follows:
    - If 3-1/2 hours are allowed, that would be 210 minutes. If you have 80 objective-type questions, that would be an average of 2-1/2 minutes per question. Allow yourself no more than 2 minutes per question, or a total of 160 minutes, which will permit about 50 minutes to review.
    - If for the time allotment of 210 minutes there are 7 essay questions to answer, that would average about 30 minutes a question. Give yourself only 25 minutes per question so that you have about 35 minutes to review.

6) The most important instruction is to *read each question* and make sure you know what is wanted. The second most important instruction is to *time yourself properly* so that you answer every question. The third most important instruction is to *answer every question*. Guess if you have to but include something for each question. Remember that you will receive no credit for a blank and will probably receive some credit if you write something in answer to an essay question. If you guess a letter – say "B" for a multiple-choice question – you may have guessed right. If you leave a blank as an answer to a multiple-choice question, the examiners may respect your feelings but it will not add a point to your score. Some exams may penalize you for wrong answers, so in such cases *only*, you may not want to guess unless you have some basis for your answer.

7) Suggestions
    a. Objective-type questions
        1. Examine the question booklet for proper sequence of pages and questions
        2. Read all instructions carefully
        3. Skip any question which seems too difficult; return to it after all other questions have been answered
        4. Apportion your time properly; do not spend too much time on any single question or group of questions

5. Note and underline key words – *all, most, fewest, least, best, worst, same, opposite*, etc.
6. Pay particular attention to negatives
7. Note unusual option, e.g., unduly long, short, complex, different or similar in content to the body of the question
8. Observe the use of "hedging" words – *probably, may, most likely*, etc.
9. Make sure that your answer is put next to the same number as the question
10. Do not second-guess unless you have good reason to believe the second answer is definitely more correct
11. Cross out original answer if you decide another answer is more accurate; do not erase until you are ready to hand your paper in
12. Answer all questions; guess unless instructed otherwise
13. Leave time for review

  b. Essay questions
  1. Read each question carefully
  2. Determine exactly what is wanted. Underline key words or phrases.
  3. Decide on outline or paragraph answer
  4. Include many different points and elements unless asked to develop any one or two points or elements
  5. Show impartiality by giving pros and cons unless directed to select one side only
  6. Make and write down any assumptions you find necessary to answer the questions
  7. Watch your English, grammar, punctuation and choice of words
  8. Time your answers; don't crowd material

8) Answering the essay question

Most essay questions can be answered by framing the specific response around several key words or ideas. Here are a few such key words or ideas:

M's: manpower, materials, methods, money, management
P's: purpose, program, policy, plan, procedure, practice, problems, pitfalls, personnel, public relations

  a. Six basic steps in handling problems:
  1. Preliminary plan and background development
  2. Collect information, data and facts
  3. Analyze and interpret information, data and facts
  4. Analyze and develop solutions as well as make recommendations
  5. Prepare report and sell recommendations
  6. Install recommendations and follow up effectiveness

  b. Pitfalls to avoid
  1. *Taking things for granted* – A statement of the situation does not necessarily imply that each of the elements is necessarily true; for example, a complaint may be invalid and biased so that all that can be taken for granted is that a complaint has been registered

2. *Considering only one side of a situation* – Wherever possible, indicate several alternatives and then point out the reasons you selected the best one
3. *Failing to indicate follow up* – Whenever your answer indicates action on your part, make certain that you will take proper follow-up action to see how successful your recommendations, procedures or actions turn out to be
4. *Taking too long in answering any single question* – Remember to time your answers properly

IX. AFTER THE TEST

Scoring procedures differ in detail among civil service jurisdictions although the general principles are the same. Whether the papers are hand-scored or graded by machine we have described, they are nearly always graded by number. That is, the person who marks the paper knows only the number – never the name – of the applicant. Not until all the papers have been graded will they be matched with names. If other tests, such as training and experience or oral interview ratings have been given, scores will be combined. Different parts of the examination usually have different weights. For example, the written test might count 60 percent of the final grade, and a rating of training and experience 40 percent. In many jurisdictions, veterans will have a certain number of points added to their grades.

After the final grade has been determined, the names are placed in grade order and an eligible list is established. There are various methods for resolving ties between those who get the same final grade – probably the most common is to place first the name of the person whose application was received first. Job offers are made from the eligible list in the order the names appear on it. You will be notified of your grade and your rank as soon as all these computations have been made. This will be done as rapidly as possible.

People who are found to meet the requirements in the announcement are called "eligibles." Their names are put on a list of eligible candidates. An eligible's chances of getting a job depend on how high he stands on this list and how fast agencies are filling jobs from the list.

When a job is to be filled from a list of eligibles, the agency asks for the names of people on the list of eligibles for that job. When the civil service commission receives this request, it sends to the agency the names of the three people highest on this list. Or, if the job to be filled has specialized requirements, the office sends the agency the names of the top three persons who meet these requirements from the general list.

The appointing officer makes a choice from among the three people whose names were sent to him. If the selected person accepts the appointment, the names of the others are put back on the list to be considered for future openings.

That is the rule in hiring from all kinds of eligible lists, whether they are for typist, carpenter, chemist, or something else. For every vacancy, the appointing officer has his choice of any one of the top three eligibles on the list. This explains why the person whose name is on top of the list sometimes does not get an appointment when some of the persons lower on the list do. If the appointing officer chooses the second or third eligible, the No. 1 eligible does not get a job at once, but stays on the list until he is appointed or the list is terminated.

X. HOW TO PASS THE INTERVIEW TEST

The examination for which you applied requires an oral interview test. You have already taken the written test and you are now being called for the interview test – the final part of the formal examination.

You may think that it is not possible to prepare for an interview test and that there are no procedures to follow during an interview. Our purpose is to point out some things you can do in advance that will help you and some good rules to follow and pitfalls to avoid while you are being interviewed.

What is an interview supposed to test?

The written examination is designed to test the technical knowledge and competence of the candidate; the oral is designed to evaluate intangible qualities, not readily measured otherwise, and to establish a list showing the relative fitness of each candidate – as measured against his competitors – for the position sought. Scoring is not on the basis of "right" and "wrong," but on a sliding scale of values ranging from "not passable" to "outstanding." As a matter of fact, it is possible to achieve a relatively low score without a single "incorrect" answer because of evident weakness in the qualities being measured.

Occasionally, an examination may consist entirely of an oral test – either an individual or a group oral. In such cases, information is sought concerning the technical knowledges and abilities of the candidate, since there has been no written examination for this purpose. More commonly, however, an oral test is used to supplement a written examination.

Who conducts interviews?

The composition of oral boards varies among different jurisdictions. In nearly all, a representative of the personnel department serves as chairman. One of the members of the board may be a representative of the department in which the candidate would work. In some cases, "outside experts" are used, and, frequently, a businessman or some other representative of the general public is asked to serve. Labor and management or other special groups may be represented. The aim is to secure the services of experts in the appropriate field.

However the board is composed, it is a good idea (and not at all improper or unethical) to ascertain in advance of the interview who the members are and what groups they represent. When you are introduced to them, you will have some idea of their backgrounds and interests, and at least you will not stutter and stammer over their names.

What should be done before the interview?

While knowledge about the board members is useful and takes some of the surprise element out of the interview, there is other preparation which is more substantive. It *is* possible to prepare for an oral interview – in several ways:

1) Keep a copy of your application and review it carefully before the interview

This may be the only document before the oral board, and the starting point of the interview. Know what education and experience you have listed there, and the sequence and dates of all of it. Sometimes the board will ask you to review the highlights of your experience for them; you should not have to hem and haw doing it.

2) Study the class specification and the examination announcement

Usually, the oral board has one or both of these to guide them. The qualities, characteristics or knowledges required by the position sought are stated in these documents. They offer valuable clues as to the nature of the oral interview. For example, if the job involves supervisory responsibilities, the announcement will usually indicate that knowledge of modern supervisory methods and the qualifications of the candidate as a supervisor will be tested. If so, you can expect such questions, frequently in the form of a hypothetical situation which you are expected to solve. NEVER go into an oral without knowledge of the duties and responsibilities of the job you seek.

3) Think through each qualification required

Try to visualize the kind of questions you would ask if you were a board member. How well could you answer them? Try especially to appraise your own knowledge and background in each area, *measured against the job sought*, and identify any areas in which you are weak. Be critical and realistic – do not flatter yourself.

4) Do some general reading in areas in which you feel you may be weak

For example, if the job involves supervision and your past experience has NOT, some general reading in supervisory methods and practices, particularly in the field of human relations, might be useful. Do NOT study agency procedures or detailed manuals. The oral board will be testing your understanding and capacity, not your memory.

5) Get a good night's sleep and watch your general health and mental attitude

You will want a clear head at the interview. Take care of a cold or any other minor ailment, and of course, no hangovers.

What should be done on the day of the interview?

Now comes the day of the interview itself. Give yourself plenty of time to get there. Plan to arrive somewhat ahead of the scheduled time, particularly if your appointment is in the fore part of the day. If a previous candidate fails to appear, the board might be ready for you a bit early. By early afternoon an oral board is almost invariably behind schedule if there are many candidates, and you may have to wait. Take along a book or magazine to read, or your application to review, but leave any extraneous material in the waiting room when you go in for your interview. In any event, relax and compose yourself.

The matter of dress is important. The board is forming impressions about you – from your experience, your manners, your attitude, and your appearance. Give your personal appearance careful attention. Dress your best, but not your flashiest. Choose conservative, appropriate clothing, and be sure it is immaculate. This is a business interview, and your appearance should indicate that you regard it as such. Besides, being well groomed and properly dressed will help boost your confidence.

Sooner or later, someone will call your name and escort you into the interview room. *This is it.* From here on you are on your own. It is too late for any more preparation. But remember, you asked for this opportunity to prove your fitness, and you are here because your request was granted.

What happens when you go in?

The usual sequence of events will be as follows: The clerk (who is often the board stenographer) will introduce you to the chairman of the oral board, who will introduce you to the other members of the board. Acknowledge the introductions before you sit down. Do not be surprised if you find a microphone facing you or a stenotypist sitting by. Oral interviews are usually recorded in the event of an appeal or other review.

Usually the chairman of the board will open the interview by reviewing the highlights of your education and work experience from your application – primarily for the benefit of the other members of the board, as well as to get the material into the record. Do not interrupt or comment unless there is an error or significant misinterpretation; if that is the case, do not hesitate. But do not quibble about insignificant matters. Also, he will usually ask you some question about your education, experience or your present job – partly to get you to start talking and to establish the interviewing "rapport." He may start the actual questioning, or turn it over to one of the other members. Frequently, each member undertakes the questioning on a particular area, one in which he is perhaps most competent, so you can expect each member to participate in the examination. Because time is limited, you may also expect some rather abrupt switches in the direction the questioning takes, so do not be upset by it. Normally, a board member will not pursue a single line of questioning unless he discovers a particular strength or weakness.

After each member has participated, the chairman will usually ask whether any member has any further questions, then will ask you if you have anything you wish to add. Unless you are expecting this question, it may floor you. Worse, it may start you off on an extended, extemporaneous speech. The board is not usually seeking more information. The question is principally to offer you a last opportunity to present further qualifications or to indicate that you have nothing to add. So, if you feel that a significant qualification or characteristic has been overlooked, it is proper to point it out in a sentence or so. Do not compliment the board on the thoroughness of their examination – they have been sketchy, and you know it. If you wish, merely say, "No thank you, I have nothing further to add." This is a point where you can "talk yourself out" of a good impression or fail to present an important bit of information. Remember, *you close the interview yourself*.

The chairman will then say, "That is all, Mr. _____, thank you." Do not be startled; the interview is over, and quicker than you think. Thank him, gather your belongings and take your leave. Save your sigh of relief for the other side of the door.

How to put your best foot forward

Throughout this entire process, you may feel that the board individually and collectively is trying to pierce your defenses, seek out your hidden weaknesses and embarrass and confuse you. Actually, this is not true. They are obliged to make an appraisal of your qualifications for the job you are seeking, and they want to see you in your best light. Remember, they must interview all candidates and a non-cooperative candidate may become a failure in spite of their best efforts to bring out his qualifications. Here are 15 suggestions that will help you:

1) Be natural – Keep your attitude confident, not cocky

If you are not confident that you can do the job, do not expect the board to be. Do not apologize for your weaknesses, try to bring out your strong points. The board is interested in a positive, not negative, presentation. Cockiness will antagonize any board member and make him wonder if you are covering up a weakness by a false show of strength.

2) Get comfortable, but don't lounge or sprawl

Sit erectly but not stiffly. A careless posture may lead the board to conclude that you are careless in other things, or at least that you are not impressed by the importance of the occasion. Either conclusion is natural, even if incorrect. Do not fuss with your clothing, a pencil or an ashtray. Your hands may occasionally be useful to emphasize a point; do not let them become a point of distraction.

3) Do not wisecrack or make small talk

This is a serious situation, and your attitude should show that you consider it as such. Further, the time of the board is limited – they do not want to waste it, and neither should you.

4) Do not exaggerate your experience or abilities

In the first place, from information in the application or other interviews and sources, the board may know more about you than you think. Secondly, you probably will not get away with it. An experienced board is rather adept at spotting such a situation, so do not take the chance.

5) If you know a board member, do not make a point of it, yet do not hide it

Certainly you are not fooling him, and probably not the other members of the board. Do not try to take advantage of your acquaintanceship – it will probably do you little good.

6) Do not dominate the interview

Let the board do that. They will give you the clues – do not assume that you have to do all the talking. Realize that the board has a number of questions to ask you, and do not try to take up all the interview time by showing off your extensive knowledge of the answer to the first one.

7) Be attentive

You only have 20 minutes or so, and you should keep your attention at its sharpest throughout. When a member is addressing a problem or question to you, give him your undivided attention. Address your reply principally to him, but do not exclude the other board members.

8) Do not interrupt

A board member may be stating a problem for you to analyze. He will ask you a question when the time comes. Let him state the problem, and wait for the question.

9) Make sure you understand the question

Do not try to answer until you are sure what the question is. If it is not clear, restate it in your own words or ask the board member to clarify it for you. However, do not haggle about minor elements.

10) Reply promptly but not hastily

A common entry on oral board rating sheets is "candidate responded readily," or "candidate hesitated in replies." Respond as promptly and quickly as you can, but do not jump to a hasty, ill-considered answer.

11) Do not be peremptory in your answers

A brief answer is proper – but do not fire your answer back. That is a losing game from your point of view. The board member can probably ask questions much faster than you can answer them.

12) Do not try to create the answer you think the board member wants

He is interested in what kind of mind you have and how it works – not in playing games. Furthermore, he can usually spot this practice and will actually grade you down on it.

13) Do not switch sides in your reply merely to agree with a board member

Frequently, a member will take a contrary position merely to draw you out and to see if you are willing and able to defend your point of view. Do not start a debate, yet do not surrender a good position. If a position is worth taking, it is worth defending.

14) Do not be afraid to admit an error in judgment if you are shown to be wrong

The board knows that you are forced to reply without any opportunity for careful consideration. Your answer may be demonstrably wrong. If so, admit it and get on with the interview.

15) Do not dwell at length on your present job

The opening question may relate to your present assignment. Answer the question but do not go into an extended discussion. You are being examined for a *new* job, not your present one. As a matter of fact, try to phrase ALL your answers in terms of the job for which you are being examined.

Basis of Rating

Probably you will forget most of these "do's" and "don'ts" when you walk into the oral interview room. Even remembering them all will not ensure you a passing grade. Perhaps you did not have the qualifications in the first place. But remembering them will help you to put your best foot forward, without treading on the toes of the board members.

Rumor and popular opinion to the contrary notwithstanding, an oral board wants you to make the best appearance possible. They know you are under pressure – but they also want to see how you respond to it as a guide to what your reaction would be under the pressures of the job you seek. They will be influenced by the degree of poise you display, the personal traits you show and the manner in which you respond.

ABOUT THIS BOOK

This book contains tests divided into Examination Sections. Go through each test, answering every question in the margin. We have also attached a sample answer sheet at the back of the book that can be removed and used. At the end of each test look at the answer key and check your answers. On the ones you got wrong, look at the right answer choice and learn. Do not fill in the answers first. Do not memorize the questions and answers, but understand the answer and principles involved. On your test, the questions will likely be different from the samples. Questions are changed and new ones added. If you understand these past questions you should have success with any changes that arise. Tests may consist of several types of questions. We have additional books on each subject should more study be advisable or necessary for you. Finally, the more you study, the better prepared you will be. This book is intended to be the last thing you study before you walk into the examination room. Prior study of relevant texts is also recommended. NLC publishes some of these in our Fundamental Series. Knowledge and good sense are important factors in passing your exam. Good luck also helps. So now study this Passbook, absorb the material contained within and take that knowledge into the examination. Then do your best to pass that exam.

EXAMINATION SECTION

EXAMINATION SECTION
TEST 1

DIRECTIONS: Each question or incomplete statement is followed by several suggested answers or completions. Select the one that BEST answers the question or completes the statement. *PRINT THE LETTER OF THE CORRECT ANSWER IN THE SPACE AT THE RIGHT.*

Questions 1-6.

DIRECTIONS: Questions 1 through 6 are to be answered on the basis of the circuit diagram below. All switches are initially open.

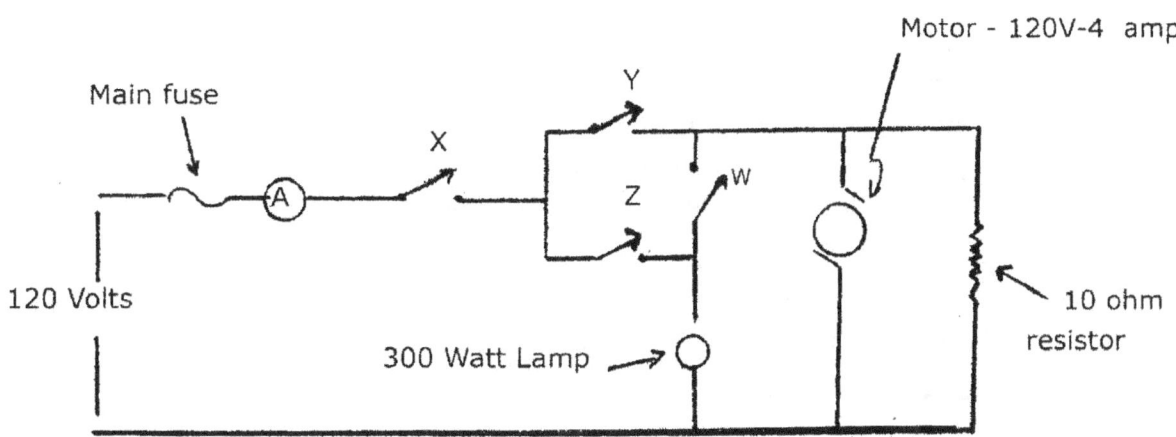

1. To light the 300 watt lamp, the following switches MUST be closed: 1.____

   A. X and Y B. Y and Z C. X and Z D. X and W

2. If all of the switches W, X, Y, and Z are closed, the following will happen: 2.____

   A. The lamp will light and the motor will rotate
   B. The lamp will light and the motor will not rotate
   C. The lamp will not light and the motor will not rotate
   D. A short circuit will occur and the main fuse will blow

3. With 120 volts applied across the 10 ohm resistor, the current drawn by the resistor is _____ amp(s). 3.____

   A. 1/12 B. 1.2 C. 12 D. 1200

4. With 120 volts applied to the 10 ohm resistor, the power used by the resistor is _____ kw. 4.____

   A. 1.44 B. 1.2 C. .144 D. .12

5. The current drawn by the 300 watt lamp when lighted should be APPROXIMATELY _____ amps. 5.____

   A. 2.5 B. 3.6 C. 25 D. 36

6. In the circuit shown, the symbol A is used to indicate a (n)

   A. ammeter   B. *and* circuit
   C. voltmeter   D. wattmeter

7. Of the following materials, the BEST conductor of electricity is

   A. iron   B. copper   C. aluminum   D. glass

8. The sum of 6'6", 5'9", and 2' 1 1/2" is

   A. 13'4 1/2"   B. 13'6 1/2"   C. 14'4 1/2"   D. 14'6 1/2"

9.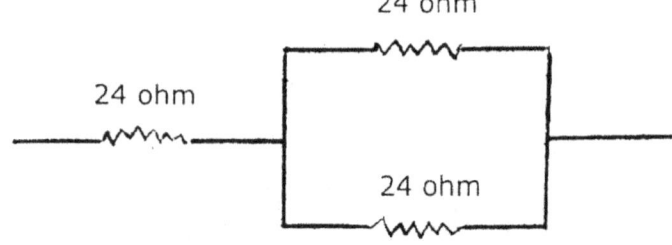

   The equivalent resistance of the three resistors shown in the sketch above is _____ ohms.

   A. 8   B. 24   C. 36   D. 72

10.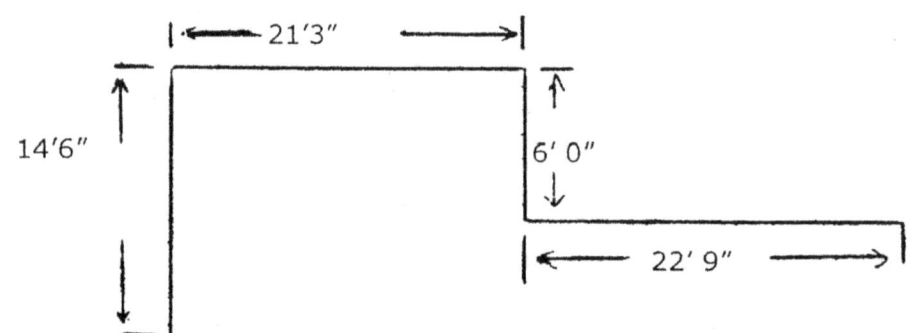

    The TOTAL length of electrical conduit that must be run along the path shown on the diagram above is

    A. 63'8"   B. 64'6"   C. 65'6"   D. 66'8"

11. Of the following electrical devices, the one that is NOT normally used in direct current electrical circuits is a (n)

    A. circuit breaker   B. double-pole switch
    C. transformer   D. inverter

12. The number of 120-volt light bulbs that should NORMALLY be connected in series across a 600-volt electric line is

    A. 1   B. 2   C. 3   D. 5

13. Of the following motors, the one that does NOT have any brushes is the _____ motor. 13._____

    A. d.c. shunt
    B. d.c. series
    C. squirrel cage induction
    D. compound

14. Of the following materials, the one that is COMMONLY used as an electric heating element in an electric heater is 14._____

    A. zinc
    B. brass
    C. terne plate
    D. nichrome

Questions 15-25.

DIRECTIONS: Questions 15 through 25 are to be answered on the basis of the instruments listed below. Each instrument is listed with an identifying number in front of it.

    1 - Hygrometer
    2 - Ammeter
    3 - Voltmeter
    4 - Wattmeter
    5 - Megger
    6 - Oscilloscope
    7 - Frequency meter
    8 - Micrometer
    9 - Vernier caliper
    10 - Wire gage
    11 - 6-foot folding rule
    12 - Architect's scale
    13 - Planimeter
    14 - Engineer's scale
    15 - Ohmmeter

15. The instrument that should be used to accurately measure the resistance of a 4,700 ohm resistor is Number 15._____

    A. 3   B. 4   C. 7   D. 15

16. To measure the current in an electrical circuit, the instrument that should be used is Number 16._____

    A. 2   B. 7   C. 8   D. 15

17. To measure the insulation resistance of a rubber-covered electrical cable, the instrument that should be used is Number 17._____

    A. 4   B. 5   C. 8   D. 15

18. An AC motor is hooked up to a power distribution box. 18._____
    In order to check the voltage at the motor terminals, the instrument that should be used is Number

    A. 2   B. 3   C. 4   D. 7

19. To measure the shaft diameter of a motor accurately to one-thousandth of an inch, the instrument that should be used is Number 19._____

    A. 8   B. 10   C. 11   D. 14

20. The instrument that should be used to determine whether 25 Hz. or 60 Hz. is present in an electrical circuit is Number 20._____

    A. 4   B. 5   C. 7   D. 8

21. Of the following, the PROPER instrument to use to determine the diameter of the conductor of a piece of electrical hook-up wire is Number

    A. 10   B. 11   C. 12   D. 14

22. The amount of electrical power being used in a balanced three-phase circuit should be measured with Number

    A. 2   B. 3   C. 4   D. 5

23. The electrical wave form at a given point in an electronic circuit can be observed with Number

    A. 2   B. 3   C. 6   D. 7

24. The PROPER instrument to use for measuring the width of a door is Number

    A. 11   B. 12   C. 13   D. 14

25. A one-inch hole with a tolerance of plus or minus three-thousandths is reamed in a steel block.
    The PROPER instrument to use to accurately check the diameter of the hole is Number

    A. 8   B. 9   C. 11   D. 14

KEY (CORRECT ANSWERS)

1. C		11. C	
2. A		12. D	
3. C		13. C	
4. A		14. D	
5. A		15. D	
6. A		16. A	
7. B		17. B	
8. C		18. B	
9. C		19. A	
10. B		20. C	

21. A
22. C
23. C
24. A
25. B

TEST 2

DIRECTIONS: Each question or incomplete statement is followed by several suggested answers or completions. Select the one that BEST answers the question or completes the statement. *PRINT THE LETTER OF THE CORRECT ANSWER IN THE SPACE AT THE RIGHT.*

1. The number of conductors required to connect a 3-phase delta connected heater bank to an electric power panel board is 1.____

   A. 2 B. 3 C. 4 D. 5

2. Of the following, the wire size that is MOST commonly used for branch lighting circuits in homes is _____ A.W.G. 2.____

   A. #12 B. #8 C. #6 D. #4

3. When installing electrical circuits, the tool that should be used to pull wire through a conduit is a 3.____

   A. mandrel B. snake
   C. rod D. pulling iron

4. Of the following AC voltages, the LOWEST voltage that a neon test lamp can detect is _____ volts. 4.____

   A. 6 B. 12 C. 80 D. 120

5. Of the following, the BEST procedure to use when storing tools that are subject to rusting is to 5.____

   A. apply a thin coating of soap onto the tools
   B. apply a light coating of oil to the tools
   C. wrap the tools in clean cheesecloth
   D. place the tools in a covered container

6. If a 3 1/2 inch long nail is required to nail wood framing members together, the nail size to use should be 6.____

   A. 2d B. 4d C. 16d D. 60d

7. Of the four motors listed below, the one that can operate only on alternating current is a(n) _____ motor. 7.____

   A. series B. shunt
   C. compound D. induction

8. The sum of 1/3 + 2/5 + 5/6 is 8.____

   A. 1 17/30 B. 1 3/5 C. 1 15/24 D. 1 5/6

9. Of the following instruments, the one that should be used to measure the state of charge of a lead-acid storage battery is a(n) 9.____

   A. ammeter B. ohmmeter
   C. hydrometer D. thermometer

10. If three 1 1/2 volt dry cell batteries are wired in series, the TOTAL voltage provided by the three batteries is _____ volts.

    A. 1.5   B. 3   C. 4.5   D. 6.0

11. Taking into account time and one-half payment for time over 40 hours of work, the gross pay of an employee who works 43 hours in a week at a rate of pay of $10.68 per hour is

    A. $427.20   B. $459.24   C. $475.26   D. $491.28

12. The sum of 0.365 + 3.941 + 10.676 + 0.784 is

    A. 13.766   B. 15.666   C. 15.756   D. 15.766

13. In order to transmit mechanical power between two rotating shafts at right angles to each other, two gears are used. Of the following, the type of gears that should be used are _____ gears.

    A. herringbone
    C. bevel
    B. spur
    D. rack and pinion

14. To properly ground the service electrical equipment in a building, a ground connection should be made to _____ the building.

    A. the waste or soil line leaving
    B. the vent line going to the exterior of
    C. any steel beam in
    D. the cold water line entering

15. The area of the triangle shown at the right is _____ square inches.
    A. 120
    B. 240
    C. 360
    D. 480

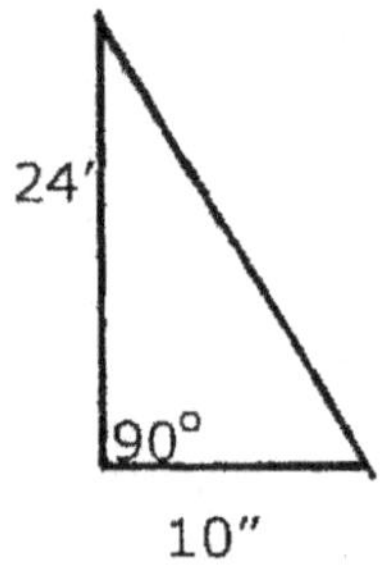

Questions 16-25.

DIRECTIONS: Questions 16 through 25 are to be answered on the basis of the tools shown on the next page. The tools are not shown to scale. Each tool is shown with an identifying number alongside it.

3 (#2)

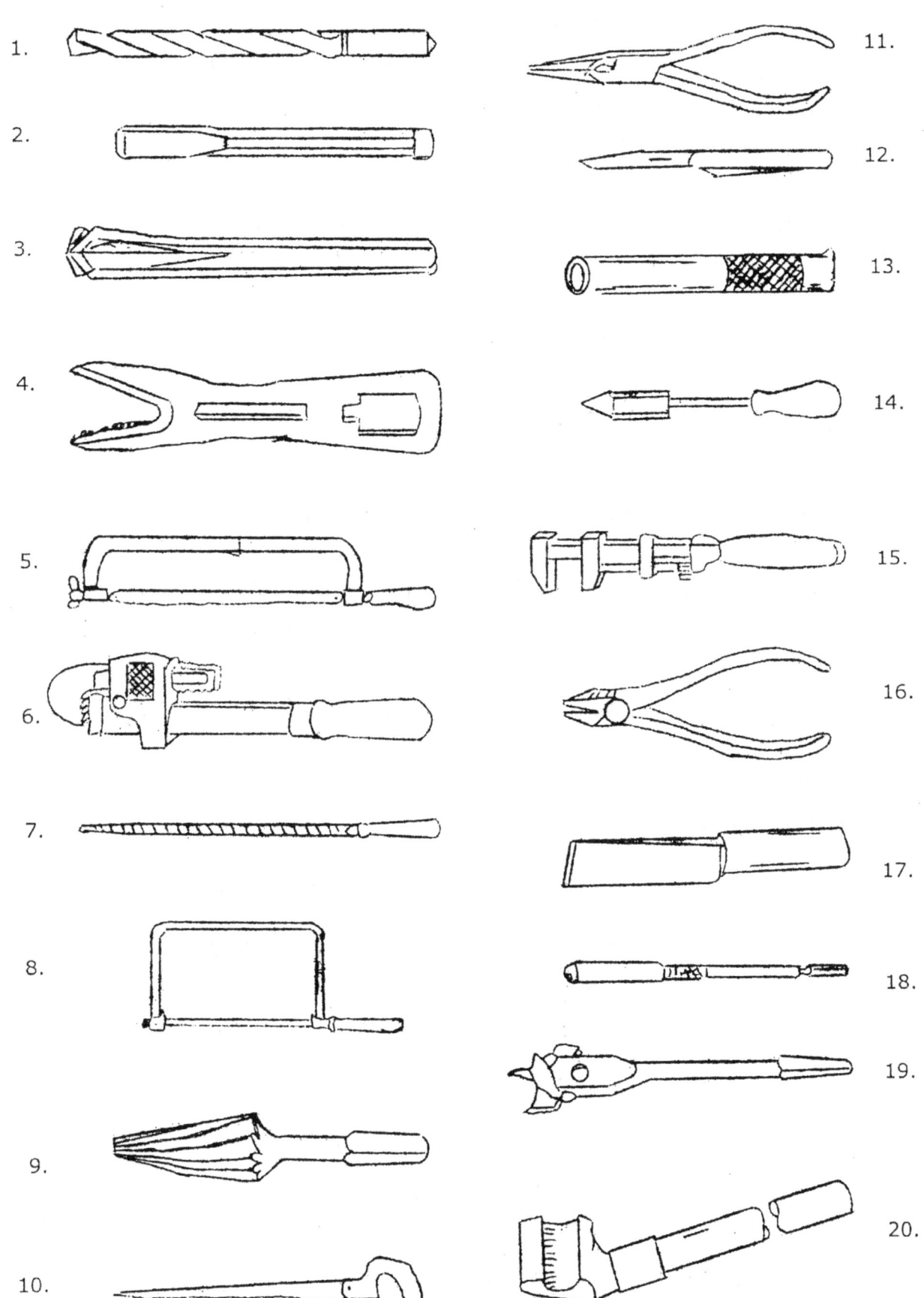

16. The tool that should be used for cutting thin wall steel conduit is Number 16._____
    A. 5 B. 8 C. 10 D. 16

17. The tool that should be used for cutting a 1 7/8 inch diameter hole in a wood joist is Number 17._____
    A. 3 B. 9 C. 14 D. 19

18. The tool that should be used for soldering splices in electrical wire is Number 18._____
    A. 3 B. 7 C. 13 D. 14

19. After cutting off a piece of 3/4 inch diameter electrical conduit, the tool that should be used for removing a burr from the inside of the conduit is Number 19._____
    A. 9 B. 11 C. 12 D. 14

20. The tool that should be used for turning a coupling onto a threaded conduit is Number 20._____
    A. 6 B. 11 C. 15 D. 16

21. The tool that should be used for cutting wood lathing in plaster walls is Number 21._____
    A. 5 B. 7 C. 10 D. 12

22. The tool that should be used for drilling a 3/8 inch diameter hole in a steel beam is Number 22._____
    A. 1 B. 2 C. 3 D. 9

23. Of the following, the BEST tool to use for stripping insulation from electrical hook-up wire is Number 23._____
    A. 11 B. 12 C. 15 D. 20

24. The tool that should be used for bending an electrical wire around a terminal post is Number 24._____
    A. 4 B. 11 C. 15 D. 16

25. The tool that should be used for cutting electrical hookup wire is Number 25._____
    A. 5 B. 12 C. 16 D. 17

KEY (CORRECT ANSWERS)

1. B
2. A
3. B
4. C
5. B

6. C
7. D
8. A
9. C
10. C

11. C
12. D
13. C
14. D
15. A

16. A
17. D
18. D
19. A
20. A

21. C
22. A
23. B
24. B
25. C

TEST 3

DIRECTIONS: Each question or incomplete statement is followed by several suggested answers or completions. Select the one that BEST answers the question or completes the statement. *PRINT THE LETTER OF THE CORRECT ANSWER IN THE SPACE AT THE RIGHT.*

1. An electric circuit has current flowing through it. The panel board switch feeding the circuit is opened, causing arcing across the switch contacts.
Generally, this arcing is caused by

    A. a lack of energy storage in the circuit
    B. electrical energy stored by a capacitor
    C. electrical energy stored by a resistor
    D. magnetic energy induced by an inductance

    1._____

2. MOST filter capacitors in radios have a capacity rating given in

    A. microvolts B. milliamps
    C. millihenries D. microfarads

    2._____

3. Of the following, the electrical wire size that is COMMONLY used for telephone circuits is _____ A.W.G.

    A. #6 B. #10 C. #12 D. #22

    3._____

Questions 4-9.

DIRECTIONS: Questions 4 through 9 are to be answered on the basis of the electrical circuit diagram shown below, where letters are used to identify various circuit components.

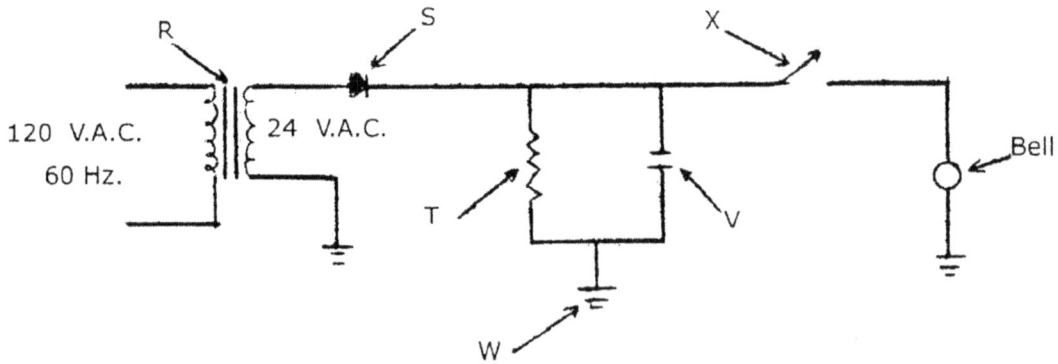

4. The device indicated by the letter R is a

    A. capacitor B. converter
    C. resistor D. transformer

    4._____

5. The device indicated by the letter S is a

    A. transistor B. diode
    C. thermistor D. directional relay

    5._____

6. The devices indicated by the letters T and V are used together to _____ components of the secondary current.

   A. reduce the AC
   B. reduce the DC
   C. transform the AC
   D. invert the AC

7. The letter W points to a standard electrical symbol for a

   A. wire
   B. ground
   C. terminal
   D. lightning arrestor

8. Closing switch X will apply the following type of voltage to the bell:

   A. 60 Hz. AC
   B. DC
   C. pulsating AC
   D. 120 Hz. AC

9. The circuit shown contains a _____ rectifier.

   A. mercury-arc
   B. full-wave
   C. bridge
   D. half-wave

10. A bolt specified as 1/4-28 means the following:
    The

    A. bolt is 1/4 inch in diameter and has 28 threads per inch
    B. bolt is 1/4 inch in diameter and is 2.8 inches long
    C. bolt is 1/4 inch long and has 28 threads
    D. threaded portion of the bolt is 1/4 inch long and has 28 threads per inch

11. When cutting 0.045-inch thickness sheet metal, it is BEST to use a hacksaw blade that has _____ teeth per inch.

    A. 7   B. 12   C. 18   D. 32

12. To accurately tighten a bolt to 28 foot-pounds, it is BEST to use a(n) _____ wrench.

    A. pipe   B. open end   C. box   D. torque

13. When bending a 2-inch diameter conduit, the CORRECT tool to use is a

    A. hickey
    B. pipe wrench
    C. hydraulic bender
    D. stock and die

14. When soldering two #20 A.W.G. copper wires together to form a splice, the solder that SHOULD be used is _____ solder.

    A. acid-core
    B. solid-core
    C. rosin-core
    D. liquid

15. A bathroom heating unit draws 10 amperes at 115 volts.
    The hot resistance of the heating unit should be _____ ohms.

    A. .08   B. 8   C. 11.5   D. 1150

16. Of the following materials, the one that is NOT suitable as an electrical insulator is

    A. glass   B. mica   C. rubber   D. platinum

17. An air conditioning unit is rated at 1000 watts. The unit is run for 10 hours per day, five days per week.
    If the cost for electrical energy is 5 cents per kilowatt-hour, the weekly cost for electricity should be

    A. 25¢ B. 50¢ C. $2.50 D. $25.00

18. If a fuse is protecting the circuit of a 15 ohm electric heater and it is designed to blow out at a current exceeding 10 amperes, the MAXIMUM voltage from among the following that should be applied across the terminals of the heater is _____ volts.

    A. 110 B. 120 C. 160 D. 600

19. Before opening a pneumatic hose connection, it is important to remove pressure from the hose line PRIMARILY to avoid

    A. losing air
    B. personal injury
    C. damage to the hose connection
    D. a build-up of pressure in the air compressor

20. If the scale on a shop drawing is 1/4 inch to the foot, then a part which measures 3 3/8 inches long on the drawing has an ACTUAL length of _____ feet _____ inches.

    A. 12; 6 B. 13; 6 C. 13; 9 D. 14; 9

21. The function that is USUALLY performed by a motor controller is to

    A. start and stop a motor
    B. protect a motor from a short circuit
    C. prevent bearing failure of a motor
    D. control the brush wear in a motor

22. Of the following galvanized sheet metal electrical outlet boxes, the one that is NOT a commonly used size is the _____ box.

    A. 4" square   B. 4" octagonal
    C. 4" x 2 1/8"   D. 4" x 1"

23. When soldering a transistor into a circuit, it is MOST important to protect the transistor from

    A. the application of an excess of rosin flux
    B. excessive heat
    C. the application of an excess of solder
    D. too much pressure

24. When installing BX type cable, it is important to protect the wires in the cable from the cut ends of the armored sheath.
    The APPROVED method of providing this protection is to

    A. use a fiber or plastic insulating bushing
    B. file the cut ends of the sheath smooth
    C. use a connector where the cable enters a junction box
    D. tie the wires into an Underwriter's knot

25. While lifting a heavy piece of equipment off the floor, a person should NOT   25._____

    A. twist his body
    B. grasp it firmly
    C. maintain a solid footing on the ground
    D. bend his knees

26. It is important that metal cabinets and panels that house electrical equipment should be grounded PRIMARILY in order to   26._____

    A. prevent short circuits from occurring
    B. keep all circuits at ground potential
    C. minimize shock hazards
    D. reduce the effects of electrolytic corrosion

27. A foreman explains a technical procedure to a new employee. If the employee does not understand the instructions he has received, it would be BEST if he were to   27._____

    A. follow the procedure as best he could
    B. ask the foreman to explain it to him again
    C. avoid following the procedure
    D. ask the foreman to give him other work

28. Of the following, the BEST connectors to use when mounting an electrical panel box directly onto a concrete wall are   28._____

    A. threaded studs   B. machine screws
    C. lag screws   D. expansion bolts

29. Of the following, the BEST instrument to use to measure the small gap between relay contacts is   29._____

    A. a micrometer   B. a feeler gage
    C. inside calipers   D. a plug gage

30. A POSSIBLE result of mounting a 40 ampere fuse in a fuse box for a circuit requiring a 20 ampere fuse is that the 40 ampere fuse may   30._____

    A. provide twice as much protection to the circuit from overloads
    B. blow more easily than the smaller fuse due to an overload
    C. cause serious damage to the circuit from an overload
    D. reduce power consumption in the circuit

KEY (CORRECT ANSWERS)

1.	D	16.	D
2.	D	17.	C
3.	D	18.	B
4.	D	19.	B
5.	B	20.	B
6.	A	21.	A
7.	B	22.	D
8.	B	23.	B
9.	D	24.	A
10.	A	25.	A
11.	D	26.	C
12.	D	27.	B
13.	C	28.	D
14.	C	29.	B
15.	C	30.	C

EXAMINATION SECTION
TEST 1

DIRECTIONS: Each question or incomplete statement is followed by several suggested answers or completions. Select the one that BEST answers the question or completes the statement. *PRINT THE LETTER OF THE CORRECT ANSWER IN THE SPACE AT THE RIGHT.*

1. Which of the following capacitors could be damaged by a reversal in polarity? A(n) _____ capacitor.
   - A. ceramic
   - B. paper
   - C. mica
   - D. electrolytic
   - E. vacuum

2. If the current through a resistor is 6 amperes and the voltage drop across it is 100 volts, what is the approximate value of the resistor in ohm(s)?
   - A. 1660   B. 166   C. 16.6   D. 1.66   E. 0.0166

3. What is the CORRECT use for an arbor press?
   - A. Bending sheet metal
   - B. Driving self-tapping screws
   - C. Removing screws
   - D. Removing "C" rings
   - E. Removing bearings from shafts

4. Which one of the following is a tensioning device in bulk-belt-type conveyor systems?
   _____ take-up.
   - A. Spring
   - B. Power
   - C. Hydraulic
   - D. Fluid coupled
   - E. Flexible coupled

5. When $X_L = X_C$ in a series circuit, what condition exists?
   - A. The circuit impedance is increasing
   - B. The circuit is at resonant frequency
   - C. The circuit current is minimum
   - D. The circuit has no e.m.f. at this time
   - E. None of the above

6. Which of the following pieces of information is NOT normally found on a schematic diagram?
   - A. Functional stage name
   - B. Supply voltages
   - C. Part symbols
   - D. Part values
   - E. Physical location of parts

7. When a single-phase induction motor drawing 24 amps at 120 VAC is reconnected to 240 VAC, what will be the amperage at 240 VAC? _____ amps.
   - A. 6   B. 8   C. 12   D. 24   E. 36

8. Which one of the following meters measures the SMALLEST current?

    A. Kilometer   B. Milliammeter   C. Microvoltmeter
    D. Millivoltmeter   E. Kilovoltmeter

9. If the current through a 1000-ohm resistor is 3 milliamperes, the voltage drop across the resistor is _____ volt(s).

    A. 1   B. 2.5   C. 3   D. 30   E. 300

10. The normally closed contacts of a relay are open when its solenoid is energized with VDC. The voltage at which the contacts re-close will be

    A. dependent upon the current through the contacts
    B. dependent upon the voltage applied to the contacts
    C. 24 VDC through the coil
    D. more than 24 VDC through the contacts
    E. less than 24 VDC through the coil

11. Electrical energy is converted to mechanical rotation by what component in the electric motor?

    A. Armature   B. Commutator   C. Field
    D. Start windings   E. Stator

12. Ohm's Law expresses the basic relationship of

    A. current, voltage, and resistance
    B. current, voltage, and power
    C. current, power, and resistance
    D. resistance, impedance, and voltage
    E. resistance, power, and impedance

13. In parallel circuits, the voltage is *always*

    A. variable   B. constant   C. alternating
    D. fluctuating   E. sporadic

14. Which one of the following is used as a voltage divider?

    A. Rotary converter   B. Potentiometer   C. Relay
    D. Circuit breaker   E. Voltmeter

Question 15.

Question 15 is based on the following diagram.

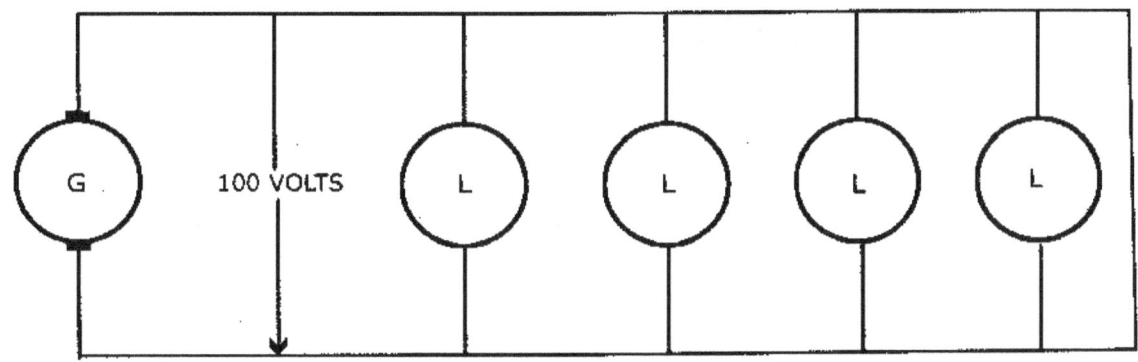

CURRENT IN EACH LAMP 1/2 AMPERE

15. What is the resistance of the entire circuit? _____ ohms. 15.____

   A. 15   B. 25   C. 35   D. 45   E. 50

16. Which one of the following tools is used to bring a bore to a specified tolerance? 16.____

   A. Tap   B. Reamer   C. Countersink
   D. Counterbore   E. Center drill

17. The primary function of a take-up pulley in a belt conveyor is to 17.____

   A. carry the belt on the return trip
   B. track the belt
   C. maintain the proper belt tension
   D. change the direction of the belt
   E. regulate the speed of the belt

Question 18.

Question 18 is based on the following diagram.

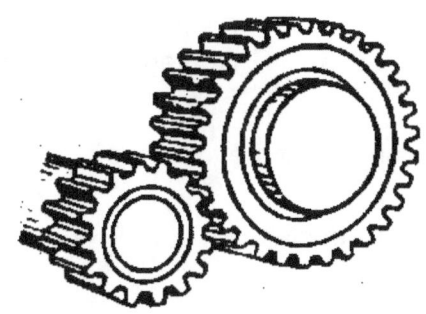

18. What is the name of the gears? 18.____

   A. Spur external   B. Spur internal   C. Helical
   D. Herringbone   D. Worm

Question 19.

Question 19 is based on the following diagram.

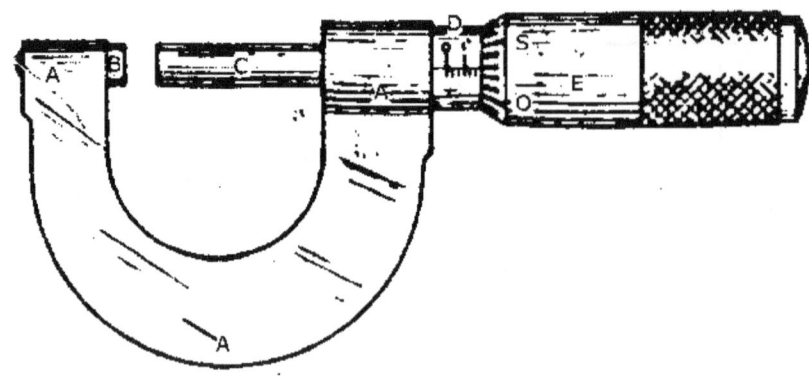

19. The part labeled D is the   19.____
    A. sleeve   B. thimble   C. frame
    D. anvil   E. pindle

Question 20.

Question 20 is based on the following symbol.

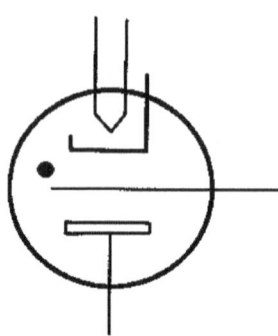

20. This symbol represents a _____ tube.   20.____
    A. thyratron vacuum   B. thyratron gas
    C. variable-mu vacuum   D. variable-mu gas
    E. vacuum photo

21. A diode can be substituted for which one of the following?   21.____
    A. Transformer   B. Relay   C. Rectifier
    D. Condenser   E. Rheostat

Question 22.

Question 22 is based on the following diagram.

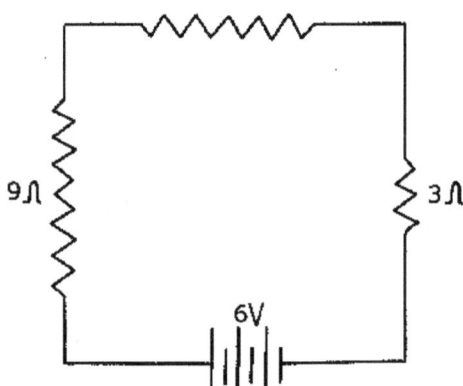

22. The rate of amperes flowing in the circuit is:

   A. .03 1/3 B. .18 C. .24
   D. .30 1/3 E. .33 1/3

   22.____

23. The firing point in a thyratron tube is *most usually* controlled by the

   A. cathode B. grid C. plate
   D. heater   E. envelope

   23.____

Questions 24-25.

Questions 24 and 25 shall be answered in accordance with the diagram below.

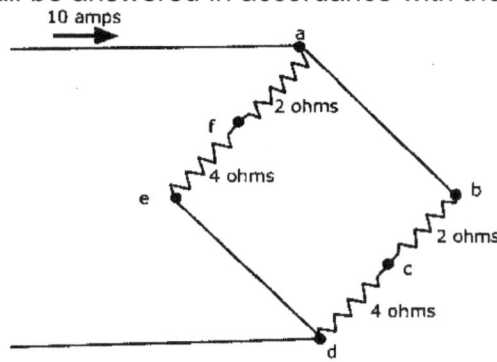

24. With reference to the above diagram, the voltage difference between points c and f is, *most nearly,* in volts,

   A. 40 B. 20 C. 10 D. 5 E. 0

   24.____

25. With reference to the above diagram, the current flowing through the resistance c d is, *most nearly,* in amperes,

   A. 10 B. 5 C. 4 D. 2 E. 1

   25.____

KEY (CORRECT ANSWERS)

1. D	6. E	11. A	16. B	21. C
2. C	7. C	12. A	17. C	22. E
3. E	8. B	13. B	18. A	23. B
4. A	9. C	14. B	19. A	24. E
5. B	10. E	15. E	20. B	25. B

EXAMINATION SECTION
TEST 1

DIRECTIONS: Each question or incomplete statement is followed by several suggested answers or completions. Select the one that BEST answers the question or completes the statement. *PRINT THE LETTER OF THE CORRECT ANSWER IN THE SPACE AT THE RIGHT.*

1. Two gears are meshed. The first gear has 20 teeth per inch and is rotating at 500 rpms. What is the speed of the second gear if it has 40 teeth per inch? _____ rpms.

   A. 500 B. 400 C. 250 D. 200

2. With two meshed gears, the first gear rotates at 100 rpms, the second gear rotates at 2000 rpms and has 10 teeth per inch.
   The first gear has _____ number of teeth per inch.

   A. 200 B. 100 C. 50 D. 150

3. Two pulleys are connected. The first pulley has a diameter of 5 inches; the second pulley has a diameter of 15 inches and rotates at 25 rpms.
   The speed of the first pulley is _____ rpms.

   A. 30 B. 75 C. 200 D. 400

4. Of two connected pulleys, the first has a radius of 10 inches and rotates at 50 rpms; the second rotates at 25 rpms.
   The diameter of the second pulley is _____ inches.

   A. 40 B. 30 C. 20 D. 10

5. Two pulleys are connected. The first pulley rotates at 75 rpms; the second pulley rotates at 100 rpms and has a diameter of 9 inches.
   The diameter of the first pulley is _____ inches.

   A. 10 B. 12 C. 15 D. 20

6. Of two connected pulleys, the first pulley has a radius of 12 inches and rotates at 60 rpms; the second pulley has a diameter of 16 inches.
   The speed of the second pulley is _____ rpms.

   A. 1000 B. 1020 C. 1040 D. 1080

7. If 16_{10} were converted to base 2, 8, and 16, the results would be _____ base 2, _____ base 8, and _____ base 16, respectively.

   A. 10000; 20; 10 B. 1000; 2000; 20
   C. 20000; 200; 20 D. 2000; 100; 10

8. Converting CAF_{16} to base 10 and base 8, the results would be _____ base 10 and _____ base 8, respectively.

   A. 2437; 2567 B. 3247; 6257
   C. 4327; 5267 D. 3427; 2657

9. Converting 101011001₂ to base 8, 10, and 16, the results would be _____ base 8, _____ base 10, and _____ base 16, respectively.

   A. 135; 45; 59
   B. 567; 435; 259
   C. 315; 245; 135
   D. 531; 345; 159

10. If 136₈ were converted to base 2, 10, and 16, the results would be _____ base 2, _____ base 10, and _____ base 16, respectively.

    A. 001011110; 94, 5E
    B. 010100110; 92; 10E
    C. 00100000; 90; 15E
    D. 011001110; 96; 20E

11. It may be correctly stated that 1000 picofarads are equal to _____ microfarads.

    A. .0001   B. .001   C. .01   D. .1

12. If 5 megohms were converted to kohms, the result would be _____ kohms.

    A. 1000   B. 2000   C. 4000   D. 5000

13. 1 nanohenry would convert to _____ millihenries.

    A. .001   B. .0001   C. .00001   D. .0000001

14. If 7 milliamps were converted to microamps, the answer would be _____ microamps.

    A. 7000   B. 700   C. 70   D. 7

15. If two resistors are in parallel and are 100 ohms each, the total resistance is

    A. 100   B. 150   C. 50   D. 10

16. In reference to the circuit in Question 15, if the first resistor has 25 volts DC, (VDC) across it, the second resistor also has 25 VDC across it, and there are no other components in the circuit except for the power source, the total circuit voltage is _____ VDC.

    A. 25   B. 50   C. 250   D. 500

17. In reference to the circuit in Question 15, if the first resistor has 1 amp on it, and the second resistor also has 1 amp on it, the total circuit amperage is _____ amps.

    A. 1   B. 2   C. 3   D. 4

18. If two resistors are in series and are 100 ohms each, the total resistance is

    A. 50   B. 100   C. 150   D. 200

19. In reference to the circuit in Question 18, if the first resistor has 25 VDC across it and the second resistor also has 25 VDC across it, the total circuit voltage is

    A. 50   B. 100   C. 200   D. 500

20. In reference to the circuit in Question 18, if the first resistor has 1 amp across it and the second resistor also has 1 amp on it, the total circuit amperage is

    A. 1   B. 5   C. 10   D. 15

21. Where two resistors are in parallel, one is 100 ohms and the other is 300 ohms. The total resistance is _____ ohms.

    A. 25 B. 35 C. 55 D. 75

22. Three resistors in series are 25 ohms, 50 ohms, and 75 ohms, respectively. The total resistance is _____ ohms.

    A. 25 B. 50 C. 100 D. 150

23. Two inductors are in parallel; the first is 50 henries and the second is also 50 henries. The total inductance is _____ henries.

    A. 25 B. 50 C. 55 D. 60

24. Two inductors are in series and the first is 50 henries; the second is 50 henries. The total inductance is _____ henries.

    A. 25 B. 50 C. 75 D. 100

25. Where two inductors are in parallel, the first is 100 henries and the second is 200 henries. The total inductance is _____ henries.

    A. 50 B. 75 C. 65 D. 100

KEY (CORRECT ANSWERS)

1. C	6. D	11. B	16. A	21. D
2. A	7. A	12. D	17. B	22. D
3. B	8. B	13. D	18. D	23. A
4. A	9. D	14. A	19. A	24. D
5. B	10. A	15. C	20. A	25. B

TEST 2

DIRECTIONS: Each question or incomplete statement is followed by several suggested answers or completions. Select the one that BEST answers the question or completes the statement. *PRINT THE LETTER OF THE CORRECT ANSWER IN THE SPACE AT THE RIGHT.*

1. Two inductors are in series; the first inductor is 100 henries and the second is 200 henries.
   The total inductance is _____ henries.

   A. 200 B. 300 C. 400 D. 500

   1._____

2. Two capacitors are in parallel; each capacitor is 30 farads.
   The total capacitance is _____ farads.

   A. 60 B. 80 C. 100 D. 200

   2._____

3. Two capacitors are in series; each capacitor is 30 farads. The total capacitance is _____ farads.

   A. 10 B. 15 C. 20 D. 25

   3._____

4. Two capacitors are in parallel; the first is 50 farads and the second is 100 farads.
   The total capacitance is _____ farads.

   A. 50 B. 100 C. 125 D. 150

   4._____

5. Two capacitors are in series; the first is 50 farads and the second is 100 farads.
   The total capacitance is _____ farads.

   A. 33.333 B. 49.999 C. 13.333 D. 25.555

   5._____

6. A resistor's color codes are orange, blue, yellow, and gold, in that order.
   The value of the resistor is _____ kohms ± _____ %.

   A. 200; 2 B. 300; 4 C. 360; 5 D. 400; 7

   6._____

7. If a resistors color codes are red, black, and blue, the value of this resistor is _____ megohms ± _____ %.

   A. 20; 20 B. 40; 80 C. 30; 30 D. 50; 50

   7._____

8. If a resistor's color codes are gray, green, black, and silver, the resistor's value is _____ ohms ± _____ %.

   A. 55; 5 B. 75; 15 C. 85; 10 D. 100; 25

   8._____

9. One complete cycle of a sinewave takes 1000 microseconds. Its frequency is _____ hertz.

   A. 500 B. 1000 C. 2000 D. 5000

   9._____

10. If one complete cycle of a squarewave takes 5 microseconds, its frequency is _____ khertz.

    A. 200 B. 500 C. 700 D. 1000

    10._____

11. What is the PRT (pulse repetition time) of a 50 hertz (hz) sinewave? _____ milliseconds. 11._____

    A. 10 B. 20 C. 40 D. 60

12. The PRT of a 20 khz sawtooth signal is _____ megahertz. 12._____

    A. 50 B. 100 C. 200 D. 500

13. If a resistor measures 10 volts and 2 amps across it, the resistance is _____ ohms. 13._____

    A. 0 B. 2 C. 5 D. 10

14. If a 30 ohm resistor measures 10 volts, the power consumed by the resistor is _____ watts. 14._____

    A. 3000 B. 5000 C. 6500 D. 7000

15. If a 50 ohm resistor measures 4 amps across, the power consumed by it is _____ watts. 15._____

    A. 200 B. 400 C. 600 D. 800

16. If a 100 ohm resistor measures 25 volts across, the current on it is _____ amps. 16._____

    A. .15 B. .25 C. .55 D. .65

Questions 17-23.

DIRECTIONS: Questions 17 through 23 are to be answered on the basis of the following diagram.

SERIES CIRCUIT

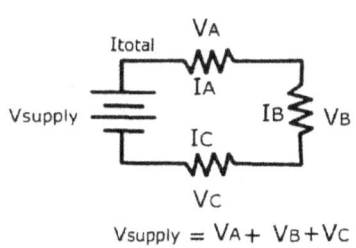

$V_{supply} = V_A + V_B + V_C$
$I_{total} = I_A = I_B = I_C$

PARALLEL CIRCUIT

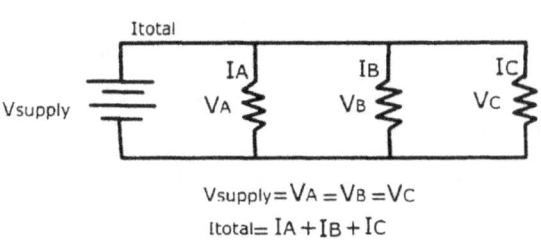

$V_{supply} = V_A = V_B = V_C$
$I_{total} = I_A + I_B + I_C$

17. In the series circuit above, if Vsupply = 100 VDC, resistor A is 10 ohms, resistor B is 50 ohms, and resistor C is 5 ohms, the total circuit current is _____ amps. 17._____

    A. 1.538 B. 1.267 C. 1.358 D. 1.823

18. In the series circuit shown above, the current across each individual resistor is _____ amps. 18._____

    A. .5 B. 1.5 C. 2.5 D. 3.5

19. In the series circuit shown above, the total power drawn by the circuit is _____ watts. 19._____

   A. 140.25   B. 150.75   C. 153.38   D. 173.38

20. In the series circuit shown above, the power drawn from each individual resistor is _____ , _____ , and _____ watts, respectively. 20._____

   A. 23.65; 118.27; 11.827
   B. 17.567; 123.27; 11.27
   C. 18.627; 145.27; 12.27
   D. 21.735; 116.87; 11.83

21. In the parallel circuit shown above, if Vsupply = 100 VDC, resistor A is 10 ohms, resistor B is 50 ohms, and resistor C is 5 ohms, the total circuit current is _____ amps. 21._____

   A. 21   B. 27   C. 32   D. 45

22. In the parallel circuit shown above, the total power drawn by the circuit is _____ watts. 22._____

   A. 1200   B. 2300   C. 2700   D. 3200

23. In the parallel circuit above, the power drawn by each individual resistor is _____ watts, respectively. 23._____

   A. 100; 200; 2000
   B. 200; 400; 5000
   C. 300; 500; 750
   D. 450; 600; 1500

24. On an 0-scope display, one cycle of a signal takes up 4 1/2 divisions and the peak-to-peak amplitude of the signal takes up 3 3/4 divisions.
   With the volts/division knob set on 5 volts and the time/division knob set to 5 microseconds, the peak-to-peak amplitude and the frequency of the signal are _____ volts and _____ khz, respectively. 24._____

   A. 15.75; 100
   B. 22.5; 200
   C. 37.5; 350
   D. 45.75; 570

25. If a signal that has a peak-to-peak amplitude of 15 volts and a frequency of 5 megaherz is to be observed on an 0-scope with one complete cycle shown, the time/division knob and volts/division knob should be set on _____ microseconds and _____ volts per division, respectively. 25._____

   A. .02; 2   B. .05; 4   C. .07; 3.5   D. 10; 7.5

KEY (CORRECT ANSWERS)

1. B	6. C	11. B	16. B	21. C
2. A	7. A	12. A	17. A	22. D
3. B	8. C	13. C	18. B	23. A
4. D	9. B	14. A	19. C	24. B
5. A	10. A	15. D	20. A	25. A

———

EXAMINATION SECTION
TEST 1

DIRECTIONS: Each question or incomplete statement is followed by several suggested answers or completions. Select the one that BEST answers the question or completes the statement. *PRINT THE LETTER OF THE CORRECT ANSWER IN THE SPACE AT THE RIGHT.*

1. A piece of equipment listed as drawing 100 watts is plugged into a 24 volt DC circuit. The MINIMUM size fuse which would handle this load is _____ amps.

   A. 2 B. 3 C. 4 D. 5

2. A resistor of 1000 ohms has 3 milliamperes passing through it. The voltage drop across the resistor is _____ volts.

   A. 3 B. 6 C. 15 D. 300

3. A certain resistor has three colored bands around it. The one nearest the end is green, the next one is orange, and the next one is red.
   The value of this register is _____ ohms.

   A. 74 B. 270 C. 5300 D. 64,000

4. An alternating voltage is applied to a capacitor.
   As the frequency of this voltage is increased, the impedance of the capacitor

   A. increases
   B. decreases
   C. remains the same
   D. increases or decreases depending on its construction

5. The one of the following that is NOT a part of a transistor is the

   A. emitter B. collector C. base D. grid

6. A 0.2 ufd capacitor is connected in series with a 0.1 ufd capacitor.
   The resultant capacity is _____ ufd.

   A. 0.067 B. 0.67 C. 0.15 D. 0.3

7. The term *Hertz* means the same as

   A. degrees Centigrade B. degrees Fahrenheit
   C. revolutions per minute D. cycles per second

8. In an electrolytic condenser, the dielectric material is

   A. mylar B. aluminum oxide
   C. paper D. sodium chloride

9. The amount by which a transformer will step up or step down a voltage is determined by its

   A. inductance B. resistance
   C. magnetic flux D. turns ratio

10. The electrolyte in a lead plate storage battery (such as that used in cars) is 10.____

    A. aluminum hydroxide
    B. sulfuric acid
    C. hydrochloric acid
    D. sodium chloride

11. A diode in an electronic circuit is used to 11.____

    A. amplify   B. oscillate   C. attenuate   D. rectify

12. The MAIN function of a filter in a power supply is to 12.____

    A. increase the voltage
    B. decrease the load
    C. smooth out the peaks of the ripple frequency
    D. protect the power transformer

13. The expression *pH* as applied to a liquid refers to its 13.____

    A. salinity
    B. specific gravity
    C. viscosity
    D. acidity/alkalinity

14. The speed of a synchronous motor is controlled by 14.____

    A. the voltage applied to it
    B. the frequency of the alternating current applied to it
    C. a mechanical governor
    D. the current it draws

15. The capacitance of a condenser is measured in 15.____

    A. oersteds   B. ohms   C. henrys   D. farads

16. The power lost in a 20-ohm resistor, with 0.25 amperes passing through it, is _____ 16.____
    watts.

    A. 0.04   B. 0.4   C. 1.25   D. 5

17. When soldering a transistor into a circuit, it is good practice to clamp a pair of long-nosed 17.____
    pliers on the lead between the transistor and the end being soldered.
    This is done to

    A. prevent the lead from moving
    B. prevent burning the fingers
    C. ground the transistor
    D. prevent the soldering iron's heat from reaching the transistor

18. The commutator of a motor should 18.____

    A. not be lubricated
    B. be lubricated with light oil
    C. be lubricated with heavy grease
    D. be lubricated with hypoid oil

19. The band of wavelengths of visible light covers 19.____

    A. 20-50 centimeters
    B. 10-50 meters
    C. 400-700 millimicrons
    D. 400-700 millimeters

20. The heat reaching the earth from the sun is transmitted by 20._____

   A. ions
   B. convection
   C. radiation
   D. cosmic rays

21. A *thermistor* is a 21._____

   A. type of thermometer
   B. high power transistor
   C. water heating device
   D. resistor with a negative temperature coefficient

22. In an AC circuit, the term *power factor* refers to the 22._____

   A. horsepower
   B. BTU per watt
   C. ratio of the resistance to the impedance
   D. kilowatts per horsepower

23. 23._____

   In the above circuit, the TOTAL resistance between points A and B is _____ ohms.

   A. 5   B. 14   C. 20   D. 45

24. Of the four gases listed below, the one that is NOT an air pollutant is 24._____

   A. carbon dioxide
   B. carbon monoxide
   C. sulfur dioxide
   D. hydrogen sulfide

25. The term *milli-roentgen* refers to a unit of 25._____

   A. x-ray radiation
   B. ultraviolet radiation
   C. reluctance
   D. inductance

26. An AC motor drawing 12 amps is plugged into a 15-amp circuit. The starting surge of the motor, however, is 18 amps. 26._____
   The PROPER type of fuse to be used in this situation is

   A. varistor
   B. thermistor
   C. fast-blow
   D. slow-blow

27. Degrees Kelvin is numerically equal to degrees 27._____

   A. Fahrenheit - 15
   B. Centigrade + 27
   C. Fahrenheit + 135
   D. Centigrade + 273

28. In the term *micromicrofarads*, the prefix *micromicro* means multiply by

   A. 10^6 B. 10^3 C. 10^{-12} D. 10^{-6}

29. One horsepower is equivalent to

   A. 276 joules
   B. 746 kilowatts
   C. 746 watts
   D. 291 calories

30. Laminated iron or steel is generally used instead of solid metal in the construction of the field and armature cores in motors and generators.
    The reason for this is to

   A. reduce eddy current losses
   B. increase the voltage
   C. decrease the flux
   D. reduce the cost

31. The instrument used to measure current flow is called a(n)

   A. wattmeter
   B. voltmeter
   C. ammeter
   D. wavemeter

32. Reversing the polarity of the voltage applied to a mica condenser will

   A. destroy it
   B. increase its capacity
   C. decrease its capacity
   D. have no effect on it

33. The *decibel* is the unit used for expressing

   A. light levels
   B. DC voltage
   C. AC current
   D. the ratio between two quantities of either electrical or sound energy

34. In a three-phase Y-connected AC power system, the voltage from leg to ground is 120 volts.
    The voltage between each pair of hot legs is _____ volts.

   A. 160   B. 180   C. 208   D. 240

35. An hygrometer is an instrument which measures

   A. humidity
   B. temperature
   C. specific gravity
   D. luminosity

36. The impedance ratio of a transformer varies _____ the turns ratio.

   A. directly with
   B. as the square of
   C. as the square root of
   D. inversely with

37. Two resistors are connected in series. The current through these resistors is 3 amperes. Resistance #1 has a value of fifty ohms; resistance #2 has a voltage drop of fifty volts across its terminals.
    The TOTAL impressed voltage (across both resistors) is _____ volts.

   A. 100   B. 150   C. 200   D. 250

38. The piece of equipment that should be used to obtain more than one voltage from a fixed voltage direct current source is a(n) 38._____

    A. multitap transformer
    B. resistance-type voltage divider
    C. autotransformer
    D. copper oxide rectifier

39. The ratio of peak to effective (rms) voltage value of a sine wave is 39._____

    A. 2 to 1   B. 1 to 2   C. .707 to 1   D. 1.414 to 1

40. Two coils are connected in series.
If there is no mutual inductance between the coils, the TOTAL inductance of the two coils is the _____ inductances. 40._____

    A. sum of the individual
    B. product of the individual
    C. product of the square roots of the two
    D. sum of the squares of the individual

41. The impedance of a coil with zero resistance is called the 41._____

    A. reluctance   B. conductance
    C. inductive reactance   D. flux

42. The ratio of the energy stored to the energy lost in a coil over a period of one cycle is called its 42._____

    A. efficiency   B. Q
    C. reactance   D. resistance

43. In a vacuum tube, the current is carried by 43._____

    A. ions   B. neutrons   C. electrons   D. molecules

44. The device used to vary the intensity of an incandescent light on a 120V AC circuit is a 44._____

    A. variable capacitor
    B. silicon controlled rectifier
    C. copper oxide rectifier
    D. rf amplifier

45. High power transistors must be mounted on *heat sinks*. The purpose of the heat sinks is to 45._____

    A. improve voltage regulation
    B. increase the transistors' output
    C. keep the transistors warm
    D. keep the transistors cool

46. The one of the following materials that has the HIGHEST conductivity is 46._____

    A. iron   B. zinc   C. copper   D. silver

47. The unit used to express the alternating current impedance of a circuit is the

    A. mho   B. farad   C. ohm   D. rel

48. A certain resistor has four colored bands on it. The fourth band is gold.
    This means that the resistor

    A. is wirewound
    B. is non-inductive
    C. has a ± 20% tolerance
    D. has a ± 5% tolerance

49. An amplifier has an output voltage waveform that does not exactly follow that of the input voltage.
    This type of distortion is called _____ distortion.

    A. modular
    B. frequency
    C. resonance
    D. amplitude

50. A parallel circuit, resonant at 1000 khz, has its value of capacity doubled and its value of inductance halved.
    Its resonant frequency now is _____ khz.

    A. 500   B. 1000   C. 1500   D. 2000

KEY (CORRECT ANSWERS)

1. D	11. D	21. D	31. C	41. C
2. A	12. C	22. C	32. D	42. B
3. C	13. D	23. B	33. D	43. C
4. B	14. B	24. A	34. C	44. B
5. D	15. D	25. A	35. A	45. D
6. A	16. C	26. D	36. B	46. D
7. D	17. D	27. D	37. C	47. C
8. B	18. A	28. C	38. B	48. D
9. D	19. C	29. C	39. D	49. D
10. B	20. C	30. A	40. A	50. B

TEST 2

DIRECTIONS: Each question or incomplete statement is followed by several suggested answers or completions. Select the one that BEST answers the question or completes the statement. *PRINT THE LETTER OF THE CORRECT ANSWER IN THE SPACE AT THE RIGHT.*

1. A voltmeter which reads 100V full scale has a specified accuracy of 3%. It is hooked across a circuit and reads 97 volts.
   The TRUE voltage can be assumed to be somewhere between

   A. 96.7 and 97.3   B. 94 and 100
   C. 96.07 and 97.03   D. 95.5 and 98.5

   1.____

2. The product of 127.2 and .0037 is

   A. 4706.4   B. 470.64   C. .47064   D. .0047064

   2.____

3. The wind velocity at a certain location was measured four times in a 24-hour period. The readings were 32 mph, 10 mph, 16 mph, and 2 mph.
   The AVERAGE wind velocity for that day was _____ mph.

   A. 24   B. 20   C. 15   D. 13

   3.____

4. When 280 is divided by .014, the answer is

   A. .002   B. 20   C. 200   D. 20,000

   4.____

5. The square root of 289 is

   A. 1.7   B. 9.7   C. 17   D. 144.5

   5.____

6. The watts drawn by a resistive load is to be determined. To do this, a voltmeter (10V full scale) is connected across the load, and an ammeter (10 amps full scale) is connected in series with the load. Both instruments are specified as having 1% (full scale) accuracy. The voltmeter reads 9.2V; the ammeter reads 8.3 amps.
   The MOST valid value for the watts drawn is _____ watts.

   A. 76   B. 76.36   C. 76.4   D. 80

   6.____

7. The formula for converting degrees Centigrade to degrees Fahrenheit is: $°F = (9/5) \cdot (°C) + 32$.
   A temperature of 25° C is equal to

   A. 102.6° F   B. 85° F   C. 77° F   D. 43° F

   7.____

8. The prefix *kilo* means

   A. multiply by one million
   B. divide by one million
   C. multiply by one thousand
   D. divide by one hundred

   8.____

9. 2^8 is equal to

   A. 512   B. 256   C. 124   D. 82

   9.____

10. The prefix *milli* means

    A. multiply by 100
    B. divide by one thousand
    C. divide by one million
    D. multiply by one million

11. If $1/X = 1/20 + 1/20 + 1/40$, the value of X is

    A. .125   B. 8   C. 16   D. 20

12. 2×10^6 multiplied by 4×10^{-6} equals

    A. 8   B. 8×10^{-12} C. 8×10^{12} D. 8×10^3

13. 1 inch equals _____ cm.

    A. 0.62   B. 2.54   C. 3.94   D. 16.2

14. 1 kg equals

    A. 2.2 lbs.   B. 17.3 oz.   C. 0.52 lbs.   D. 12 oz.

15. 1 liter equals

    A. 3.78 quarts
    B. 1.057 quarts
    C. 1.39 pints
    D. .067 gallons

16. A circle has a radius of 10 inches. Its circumference is _____ inches.

    A. 72.3   B. 62.8   C. 31.4   D. 25

17. A right angle triangle has sides measuring 3 inches and 4 inches; its hypotenuse is 5 inches.
    The area of this triangle is _____ square inches.

    A. 6   B. 20   C. 15   D. 60

18. A square has an area of 81 square inches. The length of each side is _____ inches.

    A. 7.9   B. 9   C. 11   D. 17

19. A bottle contains 11 pints of liquid. To this bottle 1.32 pints is then added. This is an increase of

    A. 6%   B. 9%   C. 12%   D. 16%

20. A week ago a storage battery read 12.4V. Today its voltage is 8.1% less. Its voltage is now

    A. 11.4   B. 10.8   C. 9.3   D. 10.2

21. The advantage of a vacuum tube voltmeter over a regular voltmeter is that it

    A. operates on batteries
    B. operates on 120V AC
    C. has a low input impedance
    D. has a high input impedance

22. A g_m tube tester measures a vacuum tube's   22.____

   A. capacitance   B. resistance
   C. emission   D. transconductance

23. A cathode ray tube is used in a(n)   23.____

   A. audio amplifier   B. radio frequency amplifier
   C. oscilloscope   D. volt-ohm-milliammeter

24. A voltmeter is described as having *1000 ohms per volt*. The current required to produce   24.____
    full scale deflection is

   A. 1 milliampere   B. 1 ampere
   C. 20 milliamperes   D. 0.05 milliamperes

25. The PRIMARY use of a test oscilloscope is to   25.____

   A. analyze complex waveforms
   B. measure resistance
   C. measure capacitance
   D. measure DC voltages

26. A spectrophotometer is an instrument that measures   26.____

   A. photographic film density
   B. the amount of light of a particular wavelength
   C. the amount of airborne dust
   D. x-ray radiation

27. The test instrument generally known as a *multitester* will measure, among other things,   27.____

   A. temperature   B. beta radiation
   C. AC watts   D. DC milliamperes

28. A lightmeter used in measuring incident light gives readings in   28.____

   A. footcandles   B. candlepower
   C. lumens   D. foot-lamberts

29. A selenium photocell is a type known as photo-   29.____

   A. emissive   B. resistive
   C. voltaic   D. transistive

30. In wiring electronic circuits, the solder GENERALLY used is _____ solder.   30.____

   A. silver   B. acid core
   C. aluminum   D. rosin core

31. An unconscious victim of electric shock should be orally administered   31.____

   A. nothing
   B. coffee
   C. alcohol
   D. aromatic apirits of ammonia

32. Persons operating x-ray equipment should wear

    A. safety goggles
    B. insulating gloves
    C. a lead-coated apron and gloves
    D. a surgical mask

33. Harmful radiation is emitted by the element

    A. neon   B. lithium   C. platinum   D. radium

34. When a victim of electrical shock or near drowning is given artificial respiration and he does not appear to respond, the treatment should continue for at least

    A. four hours   B. fifteen minutes
    C. five minutes   D. fifteen hours

35. A person maintaining high voltage equipment should avoid wearing

    A. long hair
    B. sneakers
    C. rings and metallic watchbands
    D. eyeglasses

36. Portable AC equipment is often equipped with a three-wire cable and a three-prong male plug.
    The reason for this is to prevent

    A. radiation   B. electric shock
    C. oscillation   D. ground currents

37. Smoke is seen issuing from a piece of electronic equipment. The FIRST thing that should be done is to

    A. call the fire department
    B. pour water on it
    C. look for a fire extinguisher
    D. shut off the power

38. A match should not be used when inspecting the electrolyte level in a lead-acid battery because the cells emit

    A. nitrogen   B. hydrogen
    C. carbon dioxide   D. sulfur dioxide

39. A person feels nauseated, his mental capacity has been lowered, and he has a severe throbbing headache. It is suspected that he has been poisoned by gas, but there is no apparent odor.
    The poisonous gas is MOST likely to be

    A. sulfur dioxide   B. hydrogen cyanide
    C. carbon monoxide   D. chlorine

40. The purpose of an interlock on a piece of electronic equipment is to

   A. prevent theft of the vacuum tubes
   B. prevent electrical shock to maintenance personnel
   C. prevent rf radiation
   D. keep the equipment cool

41. An alternating voltage is applied to an inductance.
    As the frequency of the voltage is decreased, the impedance of the inductance

   A. decreases
   B. increases
   C. follows the alternating voltage
   D. remains the same

42. A 0.25 ufd condenser is connected in parallel with a 0.50 ufd condenser.
    The resultant capacity is _____ ufd.

   A. 0.167   B. 0.37   C. 0.75   D. 2.5

43. The electrolyte in a carbon-zinc dry cell is

   A. sulfuric acid   B. ammonium chloride
   C. lithium chloride   D. sodium chloride

44. A 5000-ohm resistor has a voltage of 25 volts applied to it.
    The current drawn by the resistor is

   A. 5 milliamperes   B. 5 amperes
   C. 75 milliamperes   D. 1.25 milliamperes

45. A certain resistor has three colored bands around it.
    The one nearest the end is red, the next one is gray, and the next one is yellow.
    The value of the resistor is

   A. 2.7 megaohms   B. 280,000 ohms
   C. 3270 ohms   D. 449 ohms

Questions 46-50.

DIRECTIONS: Questions 46 through 50 are to be answered on the basis of the following paragraph.

The second half of the twin triode acts as a phase modulator. The rf output of the crystal oscillator is impressed on the phase-modulator grid by means of a blocking condenser. The cathode circuit is provided with a large amount of degeneration by an un-bypassed cathode resistor. Because of this degenerative feedback, the transconductance of the triode is abnormally low, so low that the plate current is affected as much by the direct grid-plate capacitance as by the transconductance. The two effects result in plate current vectors almost 180° apart, and the total plate current is the resultant of the two components. In phase, it will be about 90° removed from the phase of the voltage impressed on the grid.

6 (#2)

46. As used in the above paragraph, the word *impressed* means MOST NEARLY 46._____
    A. applied   B. blocked   C. changed   D. detached

47. As used in the above paragraph, the word *components* refers to the 47._____
    A. blocking condenser and cathode resistor
    B. twin triode
    C. plate current vectors
    D. grid-plate capacitance

48. According to the above paragraph, degenerative feedback is obtained by means of 48._____
    A. a crystal oscillator
    B. the plate voltage
    C. an un-bypassed cathode resistor
    D. a blocking condenser

49. According to the above paragraph, the cathode resistor is 49._____
    A. very large
    B. not bypassed
    C. in series with an inductance
    D. shunted by a blocking condenser

50. According to the above paragraph, the phase angle between the grid voltage and the total plate current is APPROXIMATELY 50._____
    A. 180°   B. 90°   C. 270°   D. zero

KEY (CORRECT ANSWERS)

1. B	11. B	21. D	31. A	41. A
2. C	12. C	22. D	32. C	42. C
3. C	13. B	23. C	33. D	43. B
4. D	14. A	24. A	34. A	44. A
5. C	15. B	25. A	35. C	45. B
6. A	16. B	26. B	36. B	46. A
7. C	17. A	27. D	37. D	47. C
8. C	18. B	28. A	38. B	48. C
9. B	19. C	29. C	39. C	49. B
10. B	20. A	30. D	40. B	50. B

EXAMINATION SECTION
TEST 1

DIRECTIONS: Each question or incomplete statement is followed by several suggested answers or completions. Select the one that BEST answers the question or completes the statement. PRINT THE LETTER OF THE CORRECT ANSWER IN THE SPACE AT THE RIGHT.

1. When 60,987 is added to 27,835, the result is   1._____
   A. 80,712   B. 80,822   C. 87,712   D. 88,822

2. The sum of 693 + 787 + 946 + 355 + 731 is   2._____
   A. 3,512   B. 3,502   C. 3,412   D. 3,402

3. When 2,586 is subtracted from 3,003, the result is   3._____
   A. 417   B. 527   C. 1,417   D. 1,527

4. When 1.32 is subtracted from 52.6, the result is   4._____
   A. 3.94   B. 5.128   C. 39.4   D. 51.28

5. When 56 is multiplied by 438, the result is   5._____
   A. 840   B. 4,818   C. 24,528   D. 48,180

6. When 8.7 is multiplied by .34, the result is, most nearly,   6._____
   A. 2.9   B. 3.0   C. 29.5   D. 29.6

7. When 1/2 is divided by 2/3, the result is   7._____
   A. 1/3   B. 3/4   C. 1 1/3   D. 3

8. When 8,340 is divided by 38, the result is, most nearly   8._____
   A. 210   B. 218   C. 219   D. 220

Questions 9-11.

DIRECTIONS: Questions 9 to 11 inclusive are to be answered SOLELY on the basis of the information given below.

Assume that a certain water treatment plant has consumed quantities of chemicals E and F over a five-week period, as indicated in the following table:

Time Period	Number of 100-pound sacks consumed	
	Chemical E	Chemical F
Week 1	5	4
Week 2	7	5
Week 3	6	5
Week 4	8	6
Week 5	6	4

9. The *total* number of pounds of chemical E consumed at the end of the first three weeks is 9.____

   A. 180 B. 320 C. 1,400 D. 1,800

10. According to the table, the *most* chemicals were consumed was 10.____

    A. week 2 B. week 3 C. week 4 D. week 5

11. According to the table, the *average* number of sacks of chemical F consumed over the first four weeks was 11.____

    A. 4 B. 5 C. 6 D. 7

12. Of the following actions, the *best* one to take FIRST after smoke is seen coming from an electric control device is to 12.____

    A. shut off the power to it
    B. call the main office for advice
    C. look for a wiring diagram
    D. throw water on it

13. Of the following items, the one which would LEAST likely be included on a memorandum is the 13.____

    A. home address of the writer of the memorandum
    B. name of the writer of the memorandum
    C. subject of the memorandum
    D. names or titles of the person who will receive the memorandum

14. When testing joints for leaks in pipe lines containing natural gas, it is BEST to use 14.____

    A. water in the lines under pressure
    B. a lighted candle
    C. an aquastat
    D. soapy water

Questions 15-17.

DIRECTIONS: Questions 15 to 17 inclusive are to be answered SOLELY on the basis of the information given below.

Assume that at various hours of a typical day the amounts of chlorine residual in parts per million (ppm) at a certain water treatment plant are as shown in the following graph:

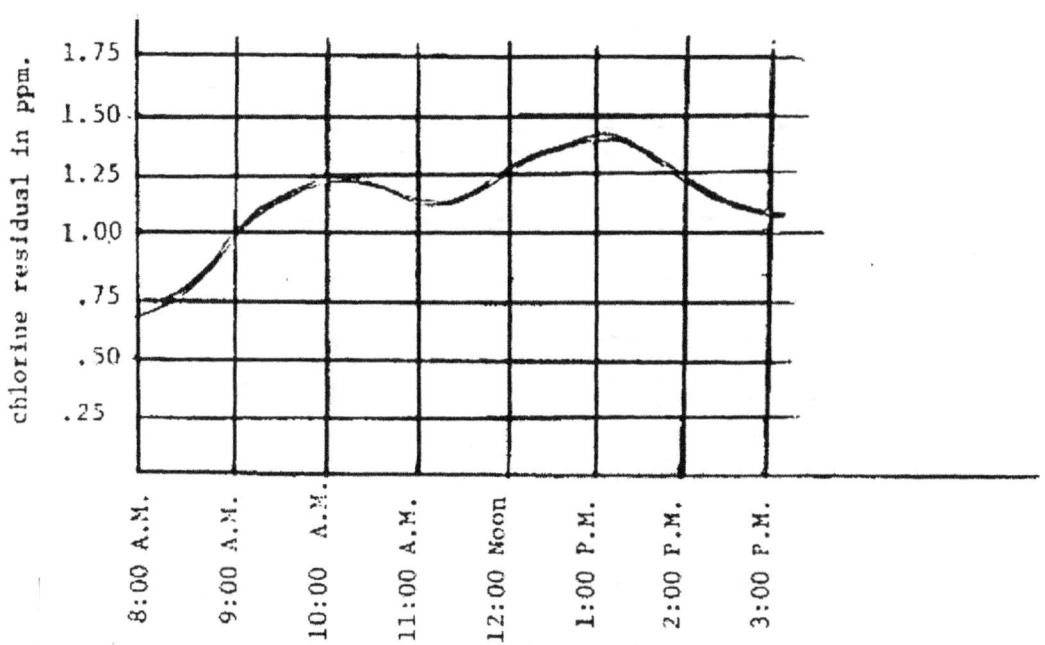

15. According to the graph, the chlorine residual measured in ppm at 9:00 A.M. was, most nearly, 15.____

    A. .70 B. .75 C. 1.00 D. 1.25

16. The maximum chlorine residual between 8:00 A.M. and 3:00 P.M. was, most nearly, 16.____

    A. .68 ppm B. 1.10 ppm C. 1.25 ppm D. 1.37 ppm

17. According to the graph, between the hour of 12:00 Noon and 1:00 P.M., the chlorine residual was 17.____

    A. always increasing
    B. always decreasing
    C. increasing, then decreasing
    D. decreasing, then increasing

18. Of the following statements concerning the use and care of wooden ladders, the *one* which is *TRUE* is that 18.____

    A. a light oil should be applied to the rungs to preserve the wood
    B. each rung should be sharply struck with a metal hammer to test its soundness before using it
    C. ladders should be stored in a warm damp area to prevent the wood from getting brittle
    D. tops of ordinary stepladders should not be used as steps

19. It is *poor* practice to use gasoline to clean metal parts that are coated with grease *PRIMARILY* because gasoline 19.____

    A. contains lead which is harmful to the user
    B. is a poor solvent for grease
    C. corrodes metal
    D. vapors ignite easily

Questions 20-21.

DIRECTIONS: Questions 20 and 21 are to be answered SOLELY on the basis of the information given in the tables below.

Inventory of 100 pound bags on hand as of 1-1	
Chemical X	16 1/2
Chemical Y	12

Date	Chemical	Number of 100 pound bags used	Number of 100 pound bags received
1-5	X	8 1/2	
1-9	X	3 1/2	
1-9	Y	5	
1-16	X		8
1-18	Y	2 1/2	
1-23	X	3	
1-27	Y	4 1/2	
1-30	X		2
1-31	X	1	

Inventory of 100 pound bags on hand as of 1-31	
Chemical X	
Chemical Y	

J. Doe
Operator

2-2

20. According to the information given in the table, the number of 100-pound bags of chemical Y *on hand* as of 1-31 is

   A. 0   B. 1/2   C. 1   D. 1 1/2

20.____

21. According to the information in the table, the *total* number of pounds of chemical X consumed in the month was, most nearly,

   A. 500   B. 1,600   C. 1,800   D. 2,800

21.____

Questions 22-27.

DIRECTIONS: Questions 22 to 27 inclusive are to be answered SOLELY on the basis of the paragraph below.

FIRST AID INSTRUCTIONS

The main purpose of first aid is to put the injured person in the best possible position until medical help arrives. This includes the performance of emergency treatment for the purpose of saving a life if a doctor is not present. When a person is hurt, a crowd usually gathers around the victim. If nobody uses his head, the injured person fails to get the care he needs. You must stay calm and, most important, it is your duty to take charge at an accident. The first thing for you to do is to see, as best you can, what is wrong with the injured person. Leave the victim where he is until the nature and extent of his injury are determined. If he is unconscious he should not be moved except to lay him flat on his back if he is in some other position. Loosen the clothing of any seriously hurt person and make him as comfortable as possible. Medical help should be called as soon as possible. You should remain with the injured person and send someone else to call the doctor. You should try to make sure that the one who calls for a doctor is able to give correct information as to the location of the injured person. In order to help the physician to know what equipment may be needed in each particular case, the person making the call should give the doctor as much information about the injury as possible.

22. If nobody uses his head at the scene of an accident, there is danger that 22.____

    A. no one will get the names of all the witnesses
    B. a large crowd will gather
    C. the victim will not get the care he needs
    D. the victim will blame the City for negligence

23. When an accident occurs, the FIRST thing you should do is 23.____

    A. call a doctor
    B. loosen the clothing of the injured person
    C. notify the victim's family
    D. try to find out what is wrong with the injured person

24. If you do NOT know the extent and nature of the victim's injuries, you should 24.____

    A. let the injured person lie where he is
    B. immediately take the victim to a hospital yourself
    C. help the injured person to his feet to see if he can walk
    D. have the injured person sit up on the ground while you examine him

25. If the injured person is breathing and unconscious, you should 25.____

    A. get some hot liquid such as coffee or tea in to him
    B. give him artificial respiration
    C. lift up his head to try to stimulate blood circulation
    D. see that he lies flat on his back

26. If it is necessary to call a doctor, you should 26.___

    A. go and make the call yourself since you have all the information
    B. find out who the victim's family doctor is before making the call
    C. have someone else make the call who knows the location of the victim
    D. find out which doctor the victim can afford

27. It is important for the caller to give the doctor as much information as is available regarding the injury so that the doctor 27.___

    A. can bring the necessary equipment
    B. can make out an accident report
    C. will be responsible for any malpractice resulting from the first aid treatment
    D. can inform his nurse on how long he will be in the field

Questions 28-29.

DIRECTIONS: Questions 28 and 29 are to be answered *SOLELY* on the basis of the paragraph below.

When a written report must be submitted by an operator to his supervisor, the best rule is "the briefer the better." Obviously, this can be carried to extremes, since all necessary information must be included. However, the ability to write a satisfactory one-page report is an important communication skill. There are several different kinds of reports in common use. One is the form report, which is printed and merely requires the operator to fill in blanks. The greatest problems faced in completion of this report are accuracy and thoroughness. Another type of report is one that must be submitted regularly and systematically. This type of report is known as the periodic report.

28. According to the passage above, accuracy and thoroughness are the *GREATEST* problems in the completion of 28.___

    A. one-page reports   B. form reports
    C. periodic reports   D. long reports

29. According to the passage above, a good written report from an operator to his supervisor should be 29.___

    A. printed
    B. formal
    C. periodic
    D. brief

Question 30.

DIRECTIONS: The sketches below show 150-lb. chlorine cylinders stored in three different ways:

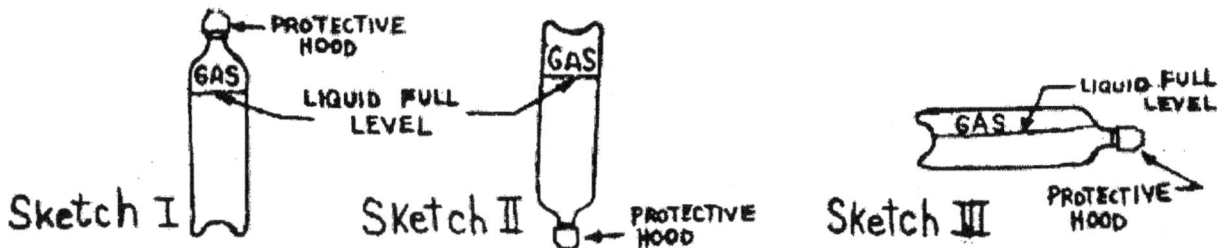

30. Recommended practice is to store a 150-lb. chlorine cylinder as shown in 30.____
    A. Sketch I *only*
    B. Sketch II *only*
    C. Sketch III *only*
    D. Sketches II and III

31. Of the following, the MOST serious defect in the installation shown below is that 31.____

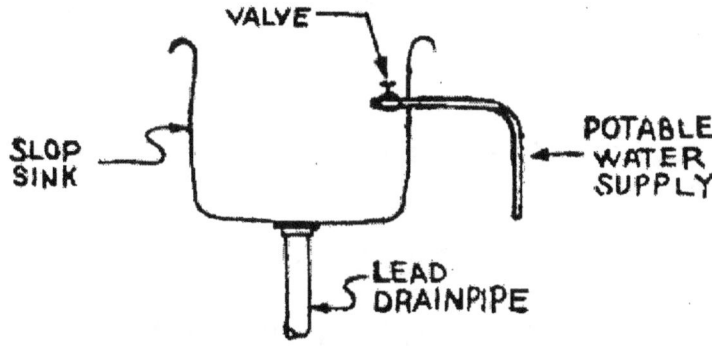

    A. the water supply should be directed downward to prevent excessive splashing over the rim
    B. the above installation may allow backflow of waste water into the water supply line
    C. lead pipes should not be used on drains from fixtures connected to the potable water supply
    D. excessive corrosion will occur on the valve if it becomes submerged

32. Of the following, the distance "x" which would be SAFEST when using the extension ladder shown in the sketch below is 32.____

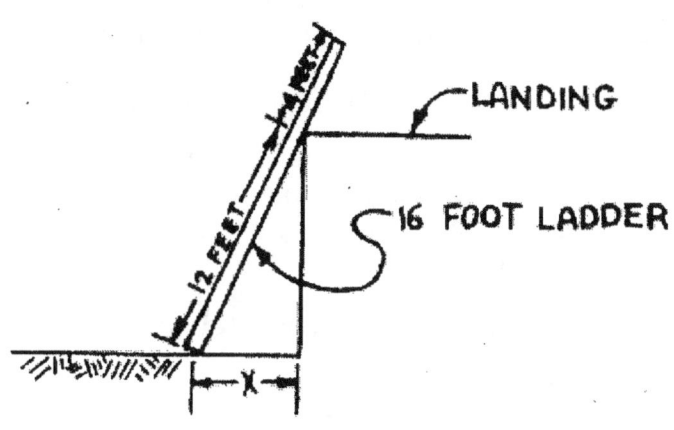

    A. 1 foot   B. 3 feet   C. 5 feet   D. 7 fee

33. Of the following statements regarding safe procedures for lifting a heavy object by yourself from the floor, the one which is FALSE is that 33.____

    A. you should keep your back as straight as possible
    B. you should bend your knees
    C. you should mainly use your back muscles in lifting
    D. your feet should be kept clear in case the object is dropped

34. It is generally not considered to be good practice to paint wood ladders. Of the following, the best reason for NOT painting wood ladders is that 34.____

    A. it may hide defects in the wood
    B. the rungs become slippery
    C. the hardware on the ladder becomes unworkable
    D. it would rub off on the surfaces against which it is resting

35. A rip saw would MOST likely be used to cut 35.____

    A. wood   B. steel   C. copper   D. aluminum

Questions 36-37.

DIRECTIONS: Questions 36 and 37 are to be answered SOLELY on the basis of the paragraph below.

NATURAL LAKES

Large lakes may yield water of exceptionally fine quality except near the shore line and in the vicinity of sewer outlets or near outlets of large streams. Therefore, minimum treatment is required. The availability of practically unlimited quantities of water is also a decided advantage. Unfortunately, however, the sewage from a city is often discharged into the same lake from which the water supply is taken. Great care must be taken in locating both the water intake and the sewer outlet so that the pollution handled by the water treatment plant is a minimum.

Sometimes the distance from the shore where dependable, satisfactory water can be found is so great that the cost of water intake facilities is prohibitive for a small municipality. In such cases, another supply must be found, or water must be obtained from a neighboring large city. Lake water is usually uniform in quality from day to day and does not vary in temperature as much as water from a river or small impounding reservoir.

36. A disadvantage of drawing a water supply from a large lake is that 36.____

    A. expensive treatment is required
    B. a limited quantity of water is available
    C. nearby cities may dump sewage into the lake
    D. the water is too cold.

37. An advantage of drawing a water supply from a large lake is that the 37.____

    A. water is uniform in quality
    B. water varies in temperature
    C. intake is distant from the shore
    D. intake may be near a sewer outlet

38. The *BEST* type of wrench to use to tighten a pipe without marring the pipe surface is   38.____

    A. pipe wrench
    B. strap wrench
    C. spanner wrench
    D. box wrench

39. Of the following statements concerning the use and care of files, the *one* which is *FALSE*   39.____
    is that

    A. files should have tight-fitting handles
    B. rasps are generally used on wood
    C. files should be protected by a light coating of oil when cutting metal
    D. files should be given a quick blow on a wood block to unclog teeth

40. A device which permits flow of a fluid in a pipe in one direction only is known as   40.____

    A. diode
    B. curb box
    C. gooseneck
    D. check valve

KEY (CORRECT ANSWERS)

1.	D	11.	B	21.	B	31.	B
2.	A	12.	A	22.	C	32.	B
3.	A	13.	A	23.	D	33.	C
4.	D	14.	D	24.	A	34.	A
5.	C	15.	C	25.	D	35.	A
6.	B	16.	D	26.	C	36.	C
7.	B	17.	A	27.	A	37.	A
8.	C	18.	D	28.	B	38.	B
9.	D	19.	D	29.	D	39.	C
10.	C	20.	A	30.	A	40.	D

TEST 2

DIRECTIONS: Each question or incomplete statement is followed by several suggested answers or completions. Select the one that *BEST* answers the question or completes the statement. *PRINT THE LETTER OF THE CORRECT ANSWER IN THE SPACE AT THE RIGHT.*

Questions 1-2.

DIRECTIONS: Questions 1 and 2 are to be answered *SOLELY* on the basis of the paragraph below.

PRECIPITATION AND RUNOFF

In the United States, the average annual precipitation is about 30 inches, of which about 21 inches is lost to the atmosphere by evaporation and transpiration. The remaining 9 inches becomes runoff into rivers and lakes. Both the precipitation and runoff vary greatly with geography and season. Annual precipitation varies from more than 100 inches in parts of the northwest to only 2 or 3 inches in parts of the southwest. In the northeastern part of the country, including New York State, the annual average precipitation is about 45 inches, of which about 22 inches becomes runoff. Even in New York State, there is some variation from place to place and considerable variation from time to time. During extremely dry years, the precipitation may be as low as 30 inches and the runoff below 10 inches. In general, there are greater variations in runoff rates from smaller watersheds. A critical water supply situation occurs when there are three or four abnormally dry years in succession.

Precipitation over the state is measured and recorded by a net-work of stations operated by the U. S. Weather Bureau. All of the precipitation records and other data such as temperature, humidity and evaporation rates are published monthly by the Weather Bureau in "Climatological Data." Runoff rates at more than 200 stream-gauging stations in the state are measured and recorded by the U. S. Geological Survey in cooperation with various state agencies. Records of the daily average flows are published annually by the U. S. Geological Survey in "Surface Water Records of New York." Copies may be obtained by writing to the Water Resources Division, United States Geological Survey, Albany, New York 23301.

1. From the above paragraphs it is *appropriate* to conclude that

    A. critical supply situations do not occur
    B. the greater the rainfall, the greater the runoff
    C. there are greater variations in runoff from larger watersheds
    D. the rainfall in the southwest is greater than the average in the country

2. From the above paragraphs, it is appropriate to conclude that

    A. an annual rainfall of about 50 inches does not occur in New York State
    B. the U. S. Weather Bureau is only interested in rainfall
    C. runoff is equal to rainfall less losses to the atmosphere
    D. information about rainfall and runoff in New York State is unavailable to the public

3. The following are diagrams of various types of bolt heads.

   The *one* of the above which is a Phillips head type is the one labelled
   A. A B. B C. C D. D

4. The appearance of frost on the outer surface of a chlorine cylinder which has been placed in service would MOST likely indicate that

   A. the cylinder is empty
   B. the gas is escaping too quickly from the cylinder
   C. there is too much pressure in the cylinder
   D. the humidity of the storage area is too high

5. One of the outer belts of a matched set of three V-belts becomes badly frayed. Of the following, the BEST course of action to take is to

   A. replace only the worn belt
   B. replace only the worn belt but put the new belt in the middle
   C. remove the worn belt, put the center belt on the end and continue running the machine
   D. replace the whole set of belts even if the other two belts show no signs of wear\

6. Of the following, the BEST type of valve to use for throttling or when the valve must be opened and closed frequently is a

   A. check valve   B. globe valve
   C. butterfly valve   D. pop valve

7. Of the following, the device which is used to measure both pressure and vacuum is the

   A. compound gage   B. aquastat
   C. pyrometer   D. thermocouple

8. Electrical energy is consumed and paid for in units of

   A. voltage   B. ampere-hours
   C. kilowatt-hours   D. watts

9. A "governor" on an engine is used to control the engine's

   A. speed   B. temperature
   C. interval of operation
   D. engaging and disengaging the "load"

10. Pressure *below* that of the atmospheric pressure is usually expressed in

    A. vacuum inches of mercury   B. inches of pressure absolute
    C. BTU's   D. gallons per minute

11. A short piece of pipe with outside threads at both ends is called a

   A. union B. nipple C. tee D. sleeve

12. Of the following, which device would MOST likely produce water hammer in a plumbing installation? A(n)

   A. relief valve B. air chamber
   C. surge tank D. quick-closing valve

13. Some portable electric tools have a third conductor in the line cord which is electrically connected to the receptacle box. The reason for this is to

   A. have a spare wire in case one power wire breaks
   B. protect the user of the tool from electrical shock
   C. strengthen the power lead so that it cannot be easily damaged
   D. allow use of the tool for extended periods of time without overheating

14. Of the following, the device which is usually used to measure the rate of flow of water in a pipe is a

   A. pressure gage B. Bourden gage
   C. manometer D. velocity meter

15. Acid, rosin fluid, or paste applied to metal surfaces to remove oxide film in preparation for soldering is known as

   A. grout B. lampblack C. plumber's soil D. flux

16. In plumbing work, a coil spring which is inserted into a drain to facilitate cleaning of the drain is known as a

   A. pipe reamer B. snake C. plunger D. spigot

17. Of the following, a pneumatic device is one that is driven or powered by

   A. air pressure B. oil pressure
   C. water pressure D. steam pressure

18. Of the following metals, the one which would MOST likely be used for an electric motor shaft is

   A. wrought iron B. hard bronze
   C. steel D. bras

19. Of the following, a rotary gear pump is BEST suited for pumping

   A. #6 fuel oil B. hot water C. sewage D. kerosene

20. The MAIN reason for using a flexible coupling to join the shafts of two pieces of machinery together is that a flexible coupling

   A. allows for slight misalignment of the two shafts
   B. can be immediately disengaged in an emergency
   C. will automatically slip when overloaded thus protecting the driver machinery
   D. allows the driven load shaft to continue rotating under its own momentum, when the driver shaft is stopped

21. Of the following, the MAIN purpose of a house trap is to

    A. provide the house drain with a cleanout
    B. prevent gases from the public sewer from entering the house plumbing system
    C. trap articles of value that are accidentally dropped into the drainage pipes
    D. eliminate the necessity for traps under all other plumbing fixtures

22. Of the following, the MAIN reason for sometimes applying bituminous coating to the interiors of steel and cast-iron pipe is that this coating

    A. increases the tensile strength of the pipe
    B. increases the shock resistance of the pipe
    C. removes any objectionable taste from the water imparted by the pipe walls
    D. protects the pipe walls from corrosion

23. The one of the following electrical devices which is most likely to be used to raise or lower A.C. voltages is a

    A. resistor   B. thermistor   C. transformer   D. circuit-breaker

24. When a metal is galvanized, it is given a coating of

    A. nickel   B. tin   C. oxide   D. zinc

25. A conduit hickey is used to

    A. measure conduit pipe   B. bend conduit pipe
    C. thread conduit pipe   D. cut conduit pipe

Questions 26-27.

DIRECTIONS: Questions 26 and 27 are to be answered SOLELY on the basis of the electrical circuit shown below.

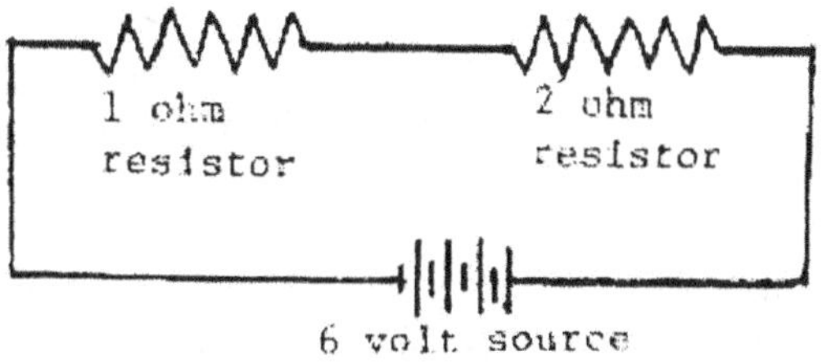

26. The circuit above is commonly known as a

    A. series circuit   B. parallel circuit
    C. short circuit   D. circuit breaker

27. The current flowing in the circuit above is

    A. 1 amp   B. 2 amps   C. 3 amps   D. 6 amps

Questions 28-30.

DIRECTIONS: Questions 28 to 30 inclusive are to be answered SOLELY on the basis of the sketches shown below.

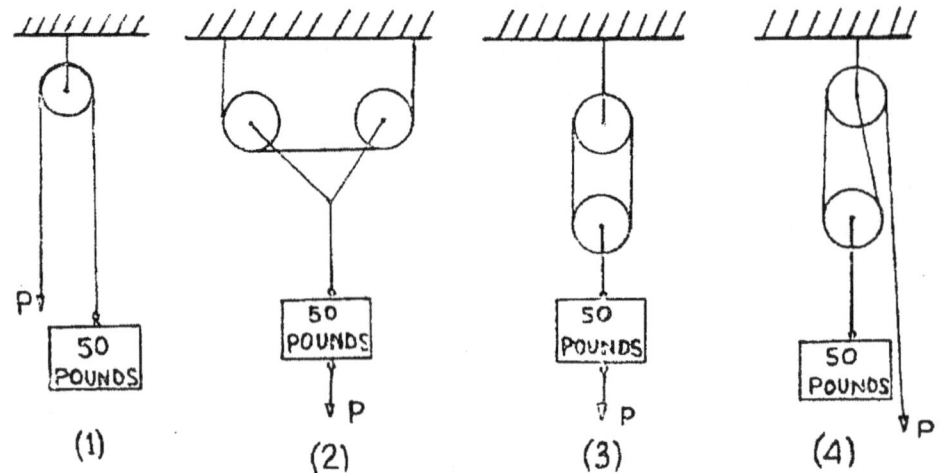

28. The two arrangements in the above diagrams which CANNOT be used to raise the load at all by applying a pull "p" as shown are setups

    A. 1 and 2   B. 2 and 3   C. 3 and 4   D. 1 and 4

29. The arrangement in the diagram above which requires the LEAST effort "p" to move the 50-pound weight is setup

    A. 1   B. 2   C. 3   D. 4

30. The effort required to hold the 50-pound weight at rest off the ground in setup (1) in the diagram above is

    A. 10 pounds   B. 25 pounds   C. 50 pounds   D. 100 pounds

31. Of the following formulas, the one which CORRECTLY shows the relationship between gage pressure and absolute pressure is

    A. Absolute pressure = gage pressure / atmospheric pressure
    B. Absolute pressure + gage pressure = atmospheric pressure
    C. Absolute pressure = gage pressure + atmospheric pressure
    D. Absolute pressure + atmospheric pressure = gage pressure

32. The weight of a gallon of water is, most nearly,

    A. 8.3 pounds   B. 16.6 pounds   C. 24.9 pounds   D. 33.2 pounds

33. Solenoid valves are usually operated

    A. thermally   B. manually   C. hydraulically   D. electrically

34. A 1/2-inch, 8-32 round-head machine screw has

    A. a diameter of 1/2 inch
    B. a length of 8 inches
    C. 8 threads per inch
    D. 32 threads per inch

35. The *MAIN* purpose for the stuffing usually found in centrifugal pump stuffing boxes is

    A. supporting the shaft
    B. controlling the rate of discharge
    C. preventing fluid leakage
    D. compensating for shaft misalignment

36. The *BEST* wrench to use on screwed valves and fittings having hexagonal shape connections is the

    A. chain wrench
    B. open-end wrench
    C. pipe wrench
    D. strap wrench

37. A tap is a tool commonly used to

    A. remove broken screws
    B. flare pipe ends
    C. cut external threads
    D. cut internal threads

38. A thread chaser is *MOST* likely to be used to

    A. rethread damaged threads
    B. remove broken taps
    C. flare tubing
    D. adjust diestocks

39. If an air-conditioning unit shorted out and caught fire, the *BEST* fire extinguisher to use would be a

    A. water extinguisher
    B. foam extinguisher
    C. carbon dioxide extinguisher
    D. soda acid extinguisher

40. Of the following, the *best* action to take to help someone whose eyes have been splashed with lye is to *FIRST*

    A. wash out the eyes with clean water
    B. wash out the eyes with a salt water solution
    C. apply a sterile dressing over the eyes
    D. do nothing to the eyes, but telephone for medical help

KEY (CORRECT ANSWERS)

1. B	11. B	21. B	31. C
2. C	12. D	22. D	32. A
3. C	13. B	23. C	33. D
4. B	14. D	24. D	34. D
5. D	15. D	25. B	35. C
6. B	16. B	26. A	36. B
7. A	17. A	27. B	37. D
8. C	18. C	28. B	38. A
9. A	19. A	29. D	39. C
10. A	20. A	30. C	40. A

EXAMINATION SECTION
TEST 1

DIRECTIONS: Each question or incomplete statement is followed by several suggested answers or completions. Select the one that BEST answers the question or completes the statement. *PRINT THE LETTER OF THE CORRECT ANSWER IN THE SPACE AT THE RIGHT.*

1. A set of conductors originating at the load side of the service equipment and supplying the main and/or one or more secondary distribution centers is commonly called a
   A. circuit   B. line   C. cable   D. feeder

   1.____

2. A 5-microfarad condenser is charged by putting 100 volts d.c. across its terminals. If this condenser is now placed across another condenser which has the same capacity rating and is identical in every other respect, the NEW voltage across these two condensers is *most nearly*
   A. 100   B. 75   C. 50   D. 25

   2.____

3. A synchronous condenser, so far as construction and appearance is concerned, *closely* resembles a(n)
   A. electrolytic condenser   B. synchronous motor
   C. synchroscope   D. wound rotor induction motor

   3.____

4. In an electric spot welding machine, the primary winding contains 200 turns of #10 wire and the secondary contains one turn made up of laminated copper sheeting.
   When the primary current is 5 amperes, the current, in amperes, passing through the metal to be welded is *approximately*
   A. 100   B. 200   C. 500   D. 1000

   4.____

5. With reference to an electric spot welding machine, the metal BEST suited to be united by spot welding is
   A. copper   B. zinc   C. lead   D. iron

   5.____

6. Two steel bars "G" and "H" have equal dimensions but one of them is a magnet and the other an ordinary piece of soft steel. In order to find out which one of the two bars is the magnet, you would touch the point midway between the ends of bar "G" with one end of bar "H". Then, if bar "H" tends to
   A. *pull* bar "G," bar "H" is not the magnet
   B. *pull* bar "G," bar "H" is the magnet
   C. *repel* bar "G," bar "H" is the magnet
   D. *repel* bar "G," bar "H" is not the magnet

   6.____

7. The MAIN purpose of a cutting fluid used in threading electrical conduits is to
   A. prevent the formation of electrolytic pockets
   B. improve the finish of the thread
   C. wash away the chips
   D. prevent the eventual formation of rust

8. If a certain electrical job requires 212 feet of ½" rigid conduit, the number of lengths that you should requisition is
   A. 16   B. 18   C. 20   D. 22

9. The number of threads per inch *commonly* used for ½" electrical conduit is
   A. 15   B. 14   C. 13   D. 12

10. For mounting a heavy pull box on a hollow tile wall, it is BEST to use
    A. lag screws
    B. masonry nails
    C. toggle bolts
    D. expansion shields

11. For mounting an outlet box on a concrete ceiling, it is BEST to use
    A. ordinary wood screws
    B. masonry nails
    C. expansion screw anchors
    D. toggle bolts

12. The electrical code states that incandescent lamps shall not be equipped with medium bases if above 1500 watts; special approved bases or other devices shall be used.
    In accordance with the above statement, the lamp base that you should use for a 750 watt incandescent lamp is the _____ base.
    A. medium   B. candelabra   C. intermediate   D. mogul

13. In order to remove rough edges after cutting, all ends of conduit should be
    A. filed   B. sanded   C. reamed   D. honed

14. Where a conduit enters a box, in order to protect the wire from abrasion, you should use an approved
    A. coupling   B. close nipple   C. locknut   D. bushing

15. The MAXIMUM number of No. 10 type R conductors permitted in a ¾" conduit is
    A. 8   B. 6   C. 4   D. 2

16. A large switch which opens automatically when the current *exceeds* a predetermined limit is called a
    A. disconnect
    B. contactor
    C. circuit breaker
    D. limit switch

17. The flux *commonly* used for soldering electrical wires is
    A. rosin   B. borax   C. zinc chloride   D. tallow

18. The cost of the electrical energy consumed by a 50-watt lamp burning for 100 hours as compared to that consumed by a 100-watt lamp burning for 50 hours is
    A. four times as much
    B. three times as much
    C. twice as much
    D. the same

19. Pneumatic tools are run by
    A. electricity
    B. steam
    C. compressed air
    D. oil

20. It is required to make a right angle turn in a conduit run in which there are already 3 quarter bends following the last pull box. The fitting BEST suited to *properly* do this is a(n)
    A. cross
    B. tee
    C. union
    D. ell

21. A 10,000 ohms resistance in an electronic timing switch burned out and must be replaced. The service manual states that this resistance should have an accuracy of 5%. This means that the value of the new resistance should differ from 10,000 ohms by NOT more than _____ ohms.
    A. 50
    B. 150
    C. 300
    D. 500

22. Of the following, the A.W.G. size of single conductor bare copper wire which has the LOWEST resistance per foot is
    A. #40
    B. #10
    C. #00
    D. #0

23. The voltage output of 6 ordinary flashlight dry cells of the zinc-carbon type, when connected in parallel with each other, will be *approximately* _____ volts.
    A. 1.5
    B. 3
    C. 9
    D. 12

24. Full load current for a 5-ohm, 20-watt resistor is
    A. 4
    B. 3
    C. 2
    D. 1

25. An auto-transformer could NOT be used to
    A. step-up voltage
    B. step-down voltage
    C. act as a choke cell
    D. change a.c. frequency

KEY (CORRECT ANSWERS)

1.	D		11.	C
2.	C		12.	D
3.	B		13.	C
4.	D		14.	D
5.	D		15.	C
6.	B		16.	C
7.	B		17.	A
8.	D		18.	D
9.	B		19.	C
10.	C		20.	D

21. D
22. C
23. A
24. C
25. D

TEST 2

DIRECTIONS: Each question or incomplete statement is followed by several suggested answers or completions. Select the one that BEST answers the question or completes the statement. *PRINT THE LETTER OF THE CORRECT ANSWER IN THE SPACE AT THE RIGHT.*

1. A resistor is connected across a supply of "E" volts. The heat produced in this resistor is proportion to I^2R. If R is reduced in value, the heat produced in this resistor now
   A. increases
   B. decreases
   C. remains the same
   D. is indeterminate

   1.____

2. A d.c. shunt generator has developed some trouble. You find that there is an open armature coil. As a *temporary* measure, you should
   A. use new brushes having a thickness of at least 3 commutator segments
   B. bridge the two commutator bars across which the open coil is connected
   C. use new brushes having a thickness of at least 4 commutator segments
   D. disconnect the open coil from the commutator

   2.____

3. A cable composed of two insulated stranded conductors laid parallel, having a common cover is called a _____ cable.
   A. twin   B. duplex   C. concentric   D. sector

   3.____

4. If two equal resistance coils are connected in parallel, the resistance of this combination is *equal* to
   A. the resistance of one coil
   B. ½ the resistance of one coil
   C. twice the resistance of one coil
   D. ¼ the resistance of one coil

   4.____

5. A condenser whose capacity is one microfarad is connected in parallel with a condenser whose capacity is 2 microfarads. This combination is equal to a single condenser having a capacity, in microfarads, of *approximately*
   A. 2/3   B. 1   C. 3   D. 3/2

   5.____

Questions 6-7.

DIRECTIONS: Questions 6 and 7 are to be answered on the basis of the diagram sketched below.

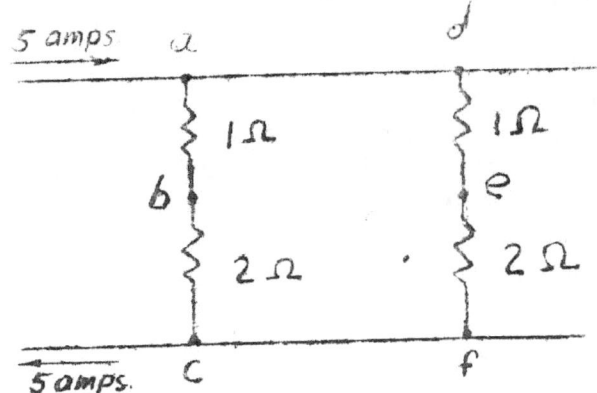

6. With reference to the diagram above, the current flowing through resistance ab is _____ amperes.
   A. 5   B. 4   C. 2½   D. 1½

7. With reference to the diagram above, the voltage difference between points b and e is _____ volt(s).
   A. 1   B. 10   C. 5   D. 0

8. The resistance of copper wire is _____ proportional to its _____.
   A. directly; cross-sectional area
   B. directly; length
   C. inversely; length
   D. inversely; diameter

9. The insulation resistance of 50 ft. of #12 BS rubber-covered wire, as compared to the insulation resistance of 100 ft. of this wire, is
   A. one-half as much
   B. the same
   C. four times as much
   D. twice as much

10. The resistance of a 150-scale voltmeter is 10,000 ohms. The power, in watts, consumed by this voltmeter when it is connected across a 100-volt circuit is
    A. 10   B. 5   C. 2.5   D. 1

11. A battery cell having an e.m.f. of 2.2 volts and an internal resistance of 0.2 ohm is connected to an external resistance 0.2 ohm. The current, in amperes, of the battery under this condition is *approximately*
    A. 15   B. 10   C. 2.5   D. 1

12. In reference to the preceding question, the efficiency, in percent, of the battery under this condition is *most nearly*
    A. 70   B. 80   C. 90   D. 100

13. During discharge, the internal resistance of a storage battery
    A. increases
    B. remains the same
    C. decreases
    D. is negative

14. The weight of a round copper bar is given by the formula, 3.14 R²LK, where R is the radius, L is the length, and K for copper is .32 lbs. per cubic inch. The weight of a round copper bar 8'4" long and 2" in diameter is *approximately*
    A. 400 lbs.   B. 300 lbs.   C. 100 lbs.   D. 50 lbs.

15. Compound d.c. generators are usually wound so as to be somewhat over-compounded. The degree of compounding is *usually* regulated by
    A. shunting more or less current from the series field
    B. shunting more or less current from the shunt field
    C. connecting it short-shunt
    D. connecting it long-shunt

16. With reference to a shunt wound d.c. generator, if the resistance of the field 16.____
    is increased to a value exceeding its critical field resistance, the generator
    A. output may exceed its name plate rating
    B. may burn out when loaded to its name plate rating
    C. output voltage will be less than its name plate rating
    D. cannot build up

17. The PROPER way to reverse the direction of rotation of a compound motor 17.____
    is to interchange the
    A. line leads   B. armature connections
    C. shunt-field connections   D. series field connections

18. In the d.c. series motor, the field 18.____
    A. has comparatively few turns of wire
    B. has comparatively many turns of wire
    C. is connected across the armature
    D. current is less than the line current

19. In the d.c. series motor, when the load torque is *decreased*, the 19.____
    A. armature rotates at a lower speed
    B. armature rotates at a higher speed
    C. current through the field is increased
    D. current through the armature is increased

20. To fasten an outlet box to a concrete ceiling, you should use 20.____
    A. wooden plugs   B. toggle bolts
    C. mollys   D. expansion bolts

21. To fasten an outlet box to a finished hollow tile wall, it is BEST to use 21.____
    A. wooden plugs   B. toggle bolts
    C. through bolts and fishplates   D. expansion bolts

Questions 22-23.

DIRECTIONS: Questions 22 and 23 are to be answered in keeping with the statement below and Figure I, which is an incomplete diagram of the connections of a fluorescent lamp. The ballast and starter are not shown.

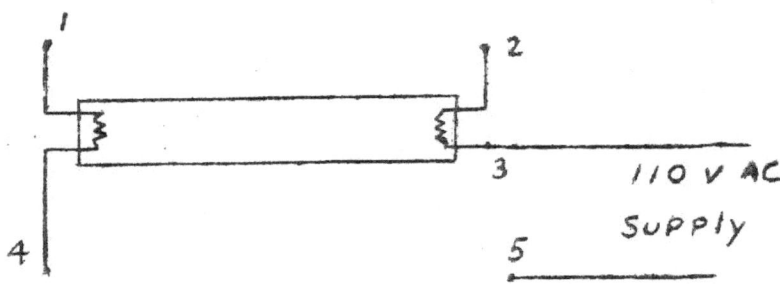

Figure I

4 (#2)

The glow type starter used to operate a fluorescent lamp is designed to act as a time switch which will connect the two filament type electrodes in each end of the lamp in series with the ballast during the short preheating period when the lamp is first turned on. The starter will then open the circuit to establish the arc.

22. From the above statement, the competent electrician should know that the starter should be shown connected between points
    A. 4 and 3   B. 1 and 2   C. 4 and 5   D. 3 and 5

23. From the above statement, the competent electrician should know that the choke of the ballast should be shown connected between points
    A. 4 and 3   B. 1 and 2   C. 4 and 5   D. 3 and 5

24. A 6000-watt 3-phase heater composed of three resistance units in delta is connected to a 3-phase, 208-volt supply. The resistance, in ohms, of each resistance unit is *most nearly*
    A. 20.8   B. 41.6   C. 83.2   D. 208

25. Based upon the data given in the preceding question, if the 3-heater resistance units are now connected in star (or wye) to a 3-phase, 208-volt supply, the power, in watts, consumed by this heater is *most nearly*
    A. 10,400   B. 6,000   C. 3,500   D. 2,000

KEY (CORRECT ANSWERS)

1.	A		11.	B
2.	B		12.	C
3.	A		13.	A
4.	B		14.	C
5.	C		15.	A
6.	C		16.	D
7.	D		17.	B
8.	B		18.	A
9.	D		19.	B
10.	D		20.	D

21.	B
22.	B
23.	C
24.	A
25.	D

TEST 3

DIRECTIONS: Each question or incomplete statement is followed by several suggested answers or completions. Select the one that BEST answers the question or completes the statement. *PRINT THE LETTER OF THE CORRECT ANSWER IN THE SPACE AT THE RIGHT.*

Questions 1-3.

DIRECTIONS: Questions 1 through 3 are to be answered on the basis of the diagram below. The sketch is a lamp independently controlled from 3 points.

1. The conductor running from the supply to switch No. 1 should be the _____ wire. 1.____
   A. blue B. white C. black D. ground

2. Switch No. 1 should be a _____ switch. 2.____
   A. single-pole B. four-way C. two-way D. three-way

3. Switch No. 2 should be a _____ switch. 3.____
   A. single-pole B. two-way C. four-way D. three-way

Questions 4-15.

DIRECTIONS: Questions 4 through 15 refer to the material given on the next page. Column I lists descriptions of work to be done. Column II lists a tool or instrument for each description listed in Column I. For each description in Column I, select the instrument or tool from Column II which is used for the particular job and write the letter which appears in front of the name of the tool or instrument.

65

Column I | Column II

4. Testing an armature for a shorted coil
5. Measure of electrical pressure
6. Measurement of electrical energy
7. Measurement of electrical power
8. Direct measurement of electrical insulation resistance
9. Direct measurement of electrical resistance (1 ohm to 10,000 ohms)
10. Direct measurement of electrical current
11. Testing to find if supply is d.c. or a.c.
12. Testing the electrolyte of battery
13. Cutting an iron bar
14. Soldering a rat-tail splice
15. A standard for checking the size of wire

Column II:
A. Neon light
B. Growler
C. Iron-vane Voltmeter
D. Ohmmeter
E. Wattmeter
F. Hot-wire Ammeter
G. Megger
H. Watthour Meter
J. Manometer
K. Cable clamp pliers
L. Pair of test lamps
M. Hack Saw
N. Hydrometer
O. Electrician's blow torch
P. American wire gage
Q. Micrometer
R. Hygrometer
S. Rip Saw

16. To transmit power economically over considerable distances, it is necessary that the voltage be high. High voltages are *readily* obtainable with _____ current.
    A. d.c.   B. a.c.   C. rectified   D. carrier

17. With reference to the preceding question, the one *favorable* economic factor in the transmission of power by using high voltages is the
    A. reduction of conductor cross section
    B. decreased amount of insulation required by the line
    C. increased I^2R loss
    D. decreased size of generating stations

18. The electric meter NOT in itself capable of measuring both d.c. and a.c. voltages is the _____ voltmeter.
    A. D'Arsonval
    B. electrodynamometer
    C. iron vane
    D. inclined-coil

19. The hot wire voltmeter
    A. is a high precision instrument
    B. is used only for d.c. circuits
    C. reads equally well on d.c. and/or a.c. circuits
    D. is used only for a.c. circuits

19.____

Questions 20-22.

DIRECTIONS: Questions 20 through 22 are to be answered on the basis of the diagram below.

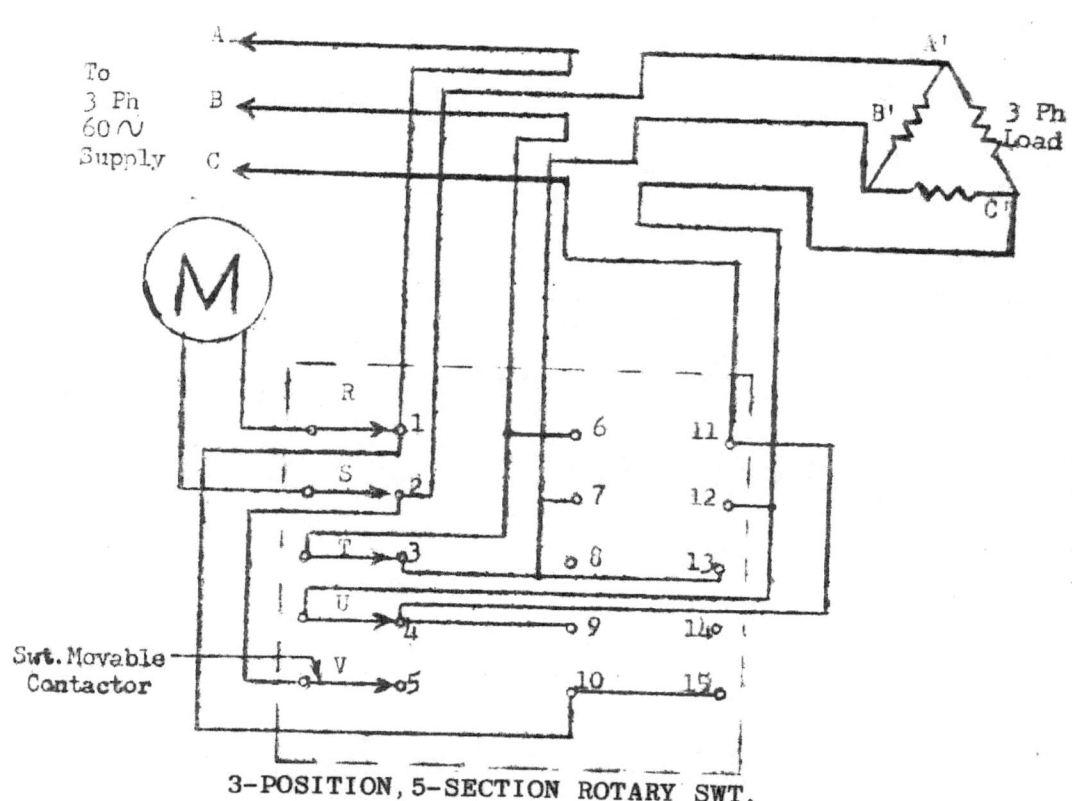

3-POSITION, 5-SECTION ROTARY SWT.

20. With switch movable contacts R, S, T, U and V in position 1, 2, 3, 4, and 5 as shown, Meter M is connected between points _____ and load is _____ connected to supply.
    A. A-A'; improperly
    B. A-A'; properly
    C. C-C'; improperly
    D. C-C'; properly

20.____

21. With switch movable contactors R, S, T, U and V in position 6, 7, 8, 9 and 10, the function of Meter M is to measure the
    A. current in line B-B'
    B. voltage in line B-B'
    C. power drawn by the load
    D. power factor of the load

21.____

22. With switch movable contactors R, S, T, U and V in position 11, 12, 13, 14 and 15, Meter M is connected between points _____ and load is _____ connected to supply.
    A. A-A'; improperly
    B. A-A'; properly
    C. C-C'; improperly
    D. C-C'; properly

23. To increase the range of d.c. ammeters, you would use a(n)
    A. current transformer
    B. inductance
    C. condenser
    D. shunt

24. To increase the range of an a.c. ammeter, the one of the following which is MOST commonly used is a(n)
    A. current transformer
    B. inductance
    C. condenser
    D. straight shunt (not U-shaped)

25. In order to properly connect a single-phase wattmeter to a circuit, you should use two
    A. current and two potential leads
    B. current leads only
    C. potential leads only
    D. current leads and two power leads

KEY (CORRECT ANSWERS)

1.	C	11.	A
2.	D	12.	N
3.	C	13.	M
4.	B	14.	O
5.	C	15.	P
6.	H	16.	B
7.	E	17.	A
8.	G	18.	A
9.	D	19.	C
10.	F	20.	B

21.	A
22.	D
23.	D
24.	A
25.	A

TEST 4

DIRECTIONS: Each question or incomplete statement is followed by several suggested answers or completions. Select the one that BEST answers the question or completes the statement. *PRINT THE LETTER OF THE CORRECT ANSWER IN THE SPACE AT THE RIGHT.*

Questions 1-2.

DIRECTIONS: Questions 1 and 2 are to be answered on the basis of the following diagram.

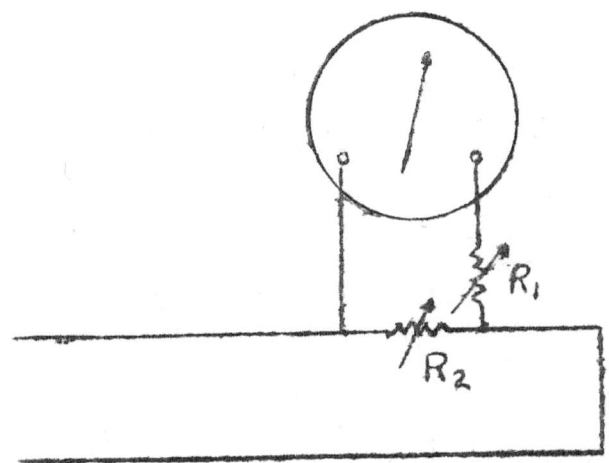

1. The above diagram represents the circuit of a d.c. ammeter. If the value of R_1 is increased while the value of R_2 remains unchanged, the
    A. deflection of the instrument is no longer proportional to the current
    B. range of the ammeter is decreased
    C. range of the ammeter remains the same
    D. range of the ammeter is increased

1.____

2. In reference to the above diagram, if the value of R_2 is decreased while the value of R_1 remains unchanged, the
    A. range of the ammeter is increased
    B. range of the ammeter is decreased
    C. range of the ammeter remains the same
    D. deflection of the instrument is no longer proportional to the current

2.____

3. In multiple-conductor armored cable construction, a color scheme is used for identifying purposes. The color-coding of a 3-conductor cable should be which one of the following?
    A. One white, one red, and one black
    B. Two black and one white
    C. Two white and one black
    D. One white, one black, and one blue

3.____

4. To properly make a short Western Union splice, the competent electrician should understand the common splicing rules. The one of the following which is NOT a common splicing rule is:
    A. Wires of the same size should be spliced together in line.
    B. A joint, or splice, must be as mechanically strong as the wire itself.
    C. A splice must provide a path for the electric current that will be as good as another wire.
    D. All splices must be mechanically and electrically secured by means of solder.

Question 5.

DIRECTIONS: Question 5 refers to the following statement.

The ampere-turns acting on a magnetic circuit are given by the product of the turns lined by the amperes flowing through these turns. Magnetomotive force tends to drive the flux through the circuit and corresponds to e.m.f. in the electric circuit. It is directly proportional to the ampere-turns and only differs from the numerical value of the ampere-turns by the constant factor 1.257, and the product of this factor and the ampere-turns equals the magnetomotive force. This unit of m.m.f. is the gilbert.

5. One pole of a d.c. motor is wound with 500 turns of wire, through which a current of 2 amperes flows. Under these conditions, the m.m.f., in gilberts, acting on this magnetic circuit is *most nearly*
    A. 1,000   B. 1,257   C. 500   D. 628

6. The flux *commonly* used for soldering electrical wire is
    A. tin chloride   B. zinc chloride
    C. rosin   D. silver amalgam

7. The operation of electrical apparatus such as generators, motors, and transformers depends *fundamentally* on induced
    A. permeance   B. e.m.f.   C. reluctance   D. permeability

8. If an inductive circuit carrying current is short-circuited, the current in the circuit will
    A. cease to flow immediately
    B. continue to flow indefinitely
    C. continue to flow for an appreciable time after the instant of short circuit
    D. increase greatly

9. With reference to a.c. supply circuits, the waves of voltage and current *ordinarily* encountered in practice are _____ waves.
    A. sine   B. triangular   C. circular   D. rectangular

Questions 10-12.

DIRECTIONS: Questions 10 through 12 are to be answered on the basis of the following diagram.

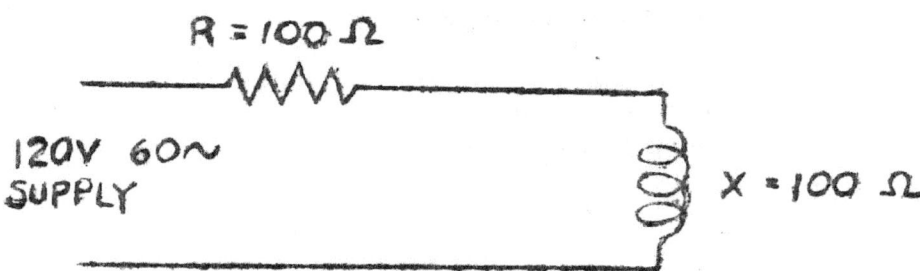

10. The value of the impedance, in ohms, of the above circuit is *most nearly*
    A. 200   B. 50   C. 150   D. 140

11. The current, in amperes, flowing in the above circuit is *most nearly*
    A. .6   B. 2.4   C. 1.2   D. .85

12. The power, in watts, consumed in the above circuit is *most nearly*
    A. 72   B. 144   C. 576   D. 36

13. The power, in watts, taken by a load connected to a three-phase circuit is *generally* expressed by
    A. EI P.F. $\sqrt{2}$ B. EI P.F.   C. $\sqrt{3}$ EI P.F.   D. EI/$\sqrt{3}$ P.F.

14. Three 100-ohm resistances are connected in wye (Y) across a 208-volt, 3-phase circuit. The line current, in amperes, is *approximately*
    A. 6.24   B. 3.6   C. 2.08   D. 1.2

15. An a.c. ammeter is calibrated to read R.M.S. values. This also means that this meter is calibrated to read the _____ value.
    A. average   B. peak   C. effective   D. square

16. An a.c. current of one ampere R.M.S. flowing through a resistance of 10 ohms has the same heating value as a d.c. current of _____ ampere(s) flowing through a _____ resistance.
    A. one; 10-ohm   B. one; 5-ohm   C. two; 10-ohm   D. five; 1-ohm

17. In the common 3-phase, 4-wire supply system, the voltage (in volts) from line to neutral is *most nearly*
    A. 110   B. 120   C. 208   D. 220

18. With reference to the preceding question, the neutral line
    A. does not carry current at any time
    B. carries current at all times
    C. has a potential difference with respect to ground of approximately zero volts
    D. has a potential difference with respect to ground of 208 volts

19. To *reverse* the direction of rotation of a repulsion motor you should
    A. move the brushes so that they cross the pole axis
    B. interchange the connection of either the main or auxiliary winding
    C. interchange the connections to the armature winding
    D. interchange the connections to the field winding

19.____

20. The ordinary direct current series motor does not operate satisfactorily with alternating current. One of the MAIN reasons for this is
    A. excessive heating due to eddy currents in the solid parts of the field structure
    B. that the armature current and field current are out of phase with each other
    C. that the field flux lags 120° in time phase with respect to the line voltage
    D. excessive heating due to the low voltage drop in the series field

20.____

21. If the full rating of a transformer is 90 KV at 90% power factor, then the KVA rating is
    A. 81   B. 90   C. 100   D. 141

21.____

22. A 10-ampere cartridge fuse provided with a navy blue label has a voltage rating, in volts, of
    A. 220   B. 250   C. 550   D. 600

22.____

23. The electrical code states that electrical metallic tubing shall not be used for interior wiring systems of more than 600 volts, nor for conductors *larger than* No.
    A. 6   B. 4   C. 2   D. 0

23.____

24. The diameter of one strand of an electrical conductor having 7 strands is .0305". The size of the conductor, in C.M., is *most nearly*
    A. 13090   B. 10380   C. 6510   D. 4107

24.____

25. To *properly* start a 15 HP d.c. compound motor, you should use a
    A. transformer   B. 4-point starting rheostat
    C. compensator   D. diverter

25.____

KEY (CORRECT ANSWERS)

1. D
2. A
3. A
4. D
5. B

6. C
7. B
8. C
9. A
10. D

11. D
12. A
13. C
14. D
15. C

16. A
17. B
18. C
19. A
20. A

21. C
22. B
23. D
24. C
25. B

TEST 5

DIRECTIONS: Each question or incomplete statement is followed by several suggested answers or completions. Select the one that BEST answers the question or completes the statement. *PRINT THE LETTER OF THE CORRECT ANSWER IN THE SPACE AT THE RIGHT.*

Questions 1-10.

DIRECTIONS: Questions 1 through 10 refer to the material given below. Column I lists definitions of terms used by the electrical code. Column II lists these terms. For each definition listed in Column I, select the term from Column II which it defines and write the letter which precedes the term.

COLUMN I

1. Current consuming equipment fixed or portable

2. That portion of a wiring system extending beyond the final overcurrent device protecting the circuit

3. Any conductors of a wiring system between the main switchboard or point of distribution and the branch circuit overcurrent device

4. Not readily accessible to persons unless special means for access are used

5. A point on the wiring system at which current is taken to supply fixtures, lamps, heaters, motors and current consuming equipment

6. The rigid steel conduit that encloses service entrance conductors

7. That portion of overhead service conductors between the last line pole and the first point of attachment to the building

8. Conductors of a wiring system between the lines of the public utility company or other source of supply and the main switchboard or point of distribution

COLUMN II

A. Mains
B. Switchboard
C. Fuse
D. Outlet
E. Service raceway
F. Feeder
G. Isolated
H. Appliances
J. Branch circuit
K. Fitting
L. Conductor
M. Enclosed
N. Surrounded
O. Service drop

1.____

2.____

3.____

4.____

5.____

6.____

7.____

8.____

9. A wire or cable or other form of metal suitable for carrying electrical energy

9.____

10. Surrounded by a case which will prevent accidental contact with live parts

10.____

Questions 11-12.

DIRECTIONS: Questions 11 and 12 are to be answered on the basis of Figure I below.

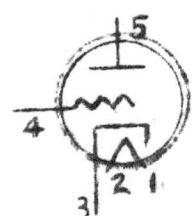

Figure I

11. The above diagram in Figure I is a *commonly* used symbol for a vacuum tube and represents which one of the following types of tubes?
    A. Triode   B. Tetrode   C. Pentode   D. Heptode

11.____

12. Tube element No. 5 is *usually* called the
    A. grid   B. plate   C. filament   D. cathode

12.____

Questions 13-14.

DIRECTIONS: Questions 13 and 14 are to be answered on the basis of Figure II below.

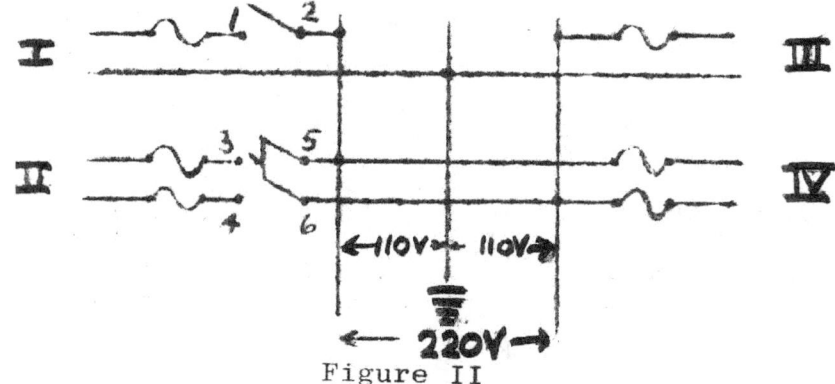

Figure II

13. Circuit No. I in the above diagram
    A. is not properly fused as it should have one fuse in each leg
    B. supplies 220 volts to the load
    C. is grounded if a pair of test lamps light when placed between point 2 and ground
    D. supplies 110 volts to the load at the board

13.____

14. Circuit No. II in the above diagram 14._____
    A. is not properly fused as it should have only one fuse in the hot leg
    B. supplies 110 volts to the load at the board
    C. is grounded if a pair of test lamps light up when placed between points 5 and 6
    D. is grounded if, with the switch in the open position, test lamps light up when placed between points 3 and 5

15. To *properly* start a 15 HP, 3-phase induction motor, you should use a 15._____
    A. shunt   B. 4-point starting rheostat
    C. compensator   D. diverter

Questions 16-25.

DIRECTIONS: Questions 16 through 25 refer to the material given below. Column I lists items which are represented by symbols listed in Column II. For each item in Column I, select the appropriate symbol from Column II which it represents and write the letter which precedes the symbol.

COLUMN I	COLUMN II	
16. Lighting panel	A.	16._____
17. Special purpose outlet	B.	17._____
18. Floor outlet	C. S_3	18._____
19. Three-way switch	D.	19._____
20. Normally closed contact	E.	20._____
21. Resistor	F.	21._____
22. Watt-hour meter	G.	22._____
23. Two-pole electrically operated contactor with blowout coil	H.	23._____
	J.	
24. Capacitor		24._____
	K.	
25. Bell		25._____
	L.	
	M.	

KEY (CORRECT ANSWERS)

1.	H		11.	A
2.	J		12.	B
3.	F		13.	D
4.	G		14.	D
5.	D		15.	C
6.	E		16.	B
7.	O		17.	D
8.	A		18.	E
9.	L		19.	C
10.	M		20.	F

21. G
22. K
23. J
24. H
25. A

———

TEST 6

DIRECTIONS: Each question or incomplete statement is followed by several suggested answers or completions. Select the one that BEST answers the question or completes the statement. *PRINT THE LETTER OF THE CORRECT ANSWER IN THE SPACE AT THE RIGHT.*

Questions 1-8.

DIRECTIONS: Questions 1 through 8 are to be answered on the basis of the figures below. Each question gives the proper figure to use with that question.

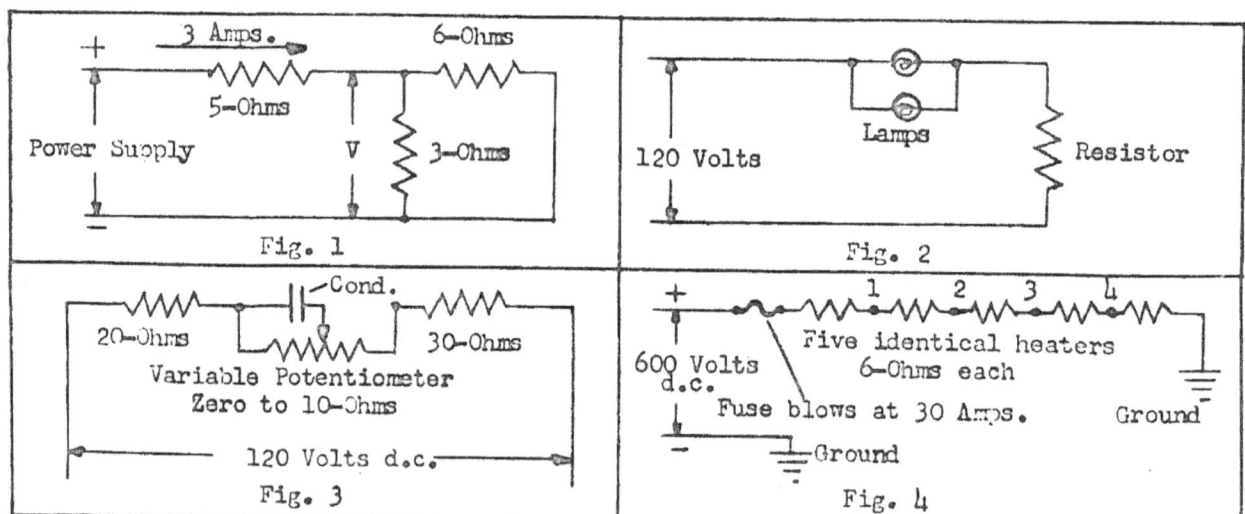

1. In Figure 1, the voltage V is _____ volts.
   A. 27   B. 9   C. 6   D. 3

2. In Figure 1, the current in the 6-ohm resistor is _____ ampere(s).
   A. 3   B. 2   C. 1.6   D. 1

3. In Figure 2, each lamp is to take 1 ampere at 20 volts. The resistor should be _____ ohms.
   A. 100   B. 80   C. 50   D. 40

4. In Figure 3, the MAXIMUM voltage which can be placed across the condenser by varying the potentiometer is _____ volts.
   A. 120   B. 60   C. 40   D. 20

5. In Figure 3, the MINIMUM voltage which can be placed across the condenser by varying the potentiometer is _____ volts.
   A. 60   B. 40   C. 20   D. zero

6. In Figure 4, the heater circuit is normally completed through the two ground connections shown. If an accidental ground occurs at point 4, then the number of heaters which will heat up is
   A. five   B. four   C. one   D. none

7. In Figure 4, the fuse will NOT blow with a ground at point
   A. 1   B. 2   C. 3   D. 4

8. In Figure 4, if a short occurs from point 2 to point 3, then the number of heaters which will heat up is
   A. five   B. four   C. two   D. none

Questions 9-16.

DIRECTIONS: Questions 9 through 16 are to be answered on the basis of the wiring diagram below. Refer to this diagram when answering these questions.

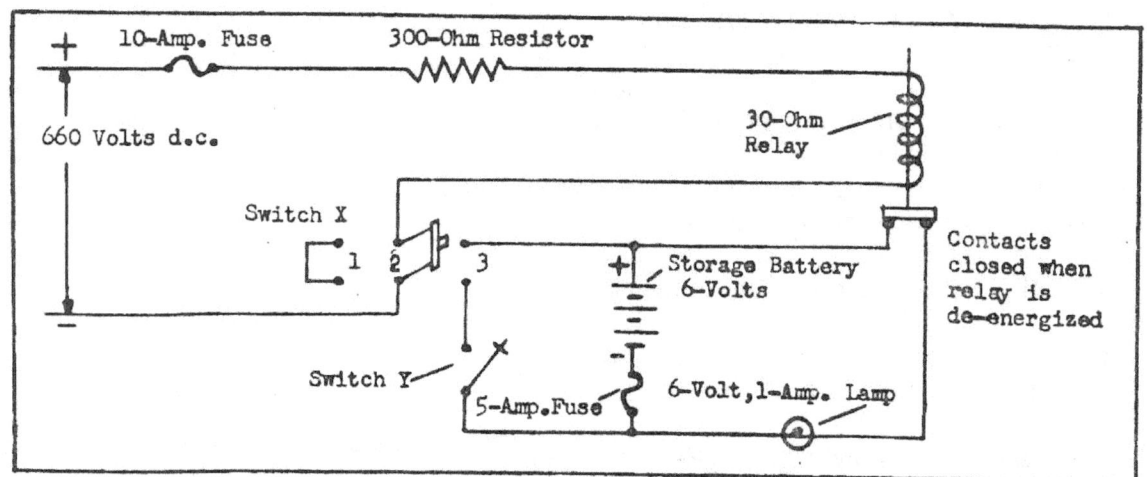

9. Throwing switch X to Position No. 1 will
   A. charge the battery
   B. energize the lamp
   C. energize the relay
   D. blow the 5-ampere fuse

10. With switch X in Position No. 1, the 10-ampere fuse will blow if a dead short occurs across the
    A. 300-ohm resistor
    B. relay coil
    C. battery
    D. lamp

11. With switch X in Position No. 2, the current through the 300-ohm resistor will be
    A. zero   B. 2 amperes   C. 2.2 amperes   D. 10 amperes

12. With switch X in Position No. 3 and switch Y open, the current taken from the battery will be
    A. zero B. 1 ampere C. 5 amperes D. 10 amperes

13. With switch Y in the open position and the relay contacts open, the
    A. lamp will be lit
    B. lamp will be dark
    C. battery will be discharging
    D. 5-ampere fuse will be overloaded

14. The battery will charge with switch X in Position No. _____ and switch Y _____.
    A. 3; closed B. 3; open C. 1; closed D. 1; open

15. With the relay contacts closed, a dead short across the lamp will
    A. blow the 10-ampere fuse
    B. blow the 5-ampere fuse
    C. not blow any fuses
    D. cause the battery to charge

16. When the switches are set to the positions which will charge the battery, the charging current will be *approximately* _____ ampere(s).
    A. ½ B. 2 C. 5 D. 10

17. The MOST important reason for NOT having a power line splice in a conduit run between boxes is that
    A. it will be impossible to pull the wires through
    B. this would be an unsafe practice
    C. the splice will heat up
    D. the splice would be hard to repair

18. Goggles would be LEAST necessary when
    A. recharging soda-acid fire extinguishers
    B. chipping stones
    C. putting electrolyte into an Edison battery
    D. scraping rubber insulation from a wire

19. A commutator and brushes will be found on a(n)
    A. alternator
    B. rotary converter
    C. squirrel-cage induction motor
    D. wound-rotor induction motor

20. In a house bell circuit, the pushbutton for ringing the bell is generally connected in the secondary of the transformer feeding the bell. One reason for this is to
    A. save power
    B. keep line voltage out of the pushbutton circuit
    C. prevent the bell from burning out
    D. prevent arcing of the vibrator contact points in the bell

KEY (CORRECT ANSWERS)

1.	C	11.	A
2.	D	12.	B
3.	C	13.	B
4.	D	14.	A
5.	D	15.	B
6.	B	16.	B
7.	D	17.	B
8.	B	18.	D
9.	C	19.	B
10.	A	20.	B

MECHANICAL APTITUDE
TOOL RECOGNITION AND USE

EXAMINATION SECTION
TEST 1

DIRECTIONS: Each question or incomplete statement below is followed by several suggested answers or completions. Select the one that BEST answers the question or completes the statement.

KEY: CORRECT ANSWERS APPEAR AT THE END OF THIS TEST.

1.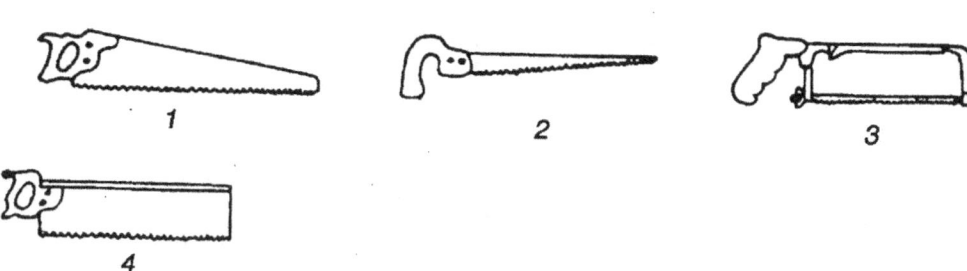

   The saw that is used principally where curved cuts are to be made is numbered

   1. 1   2. 2   3. 3   4. 4

2.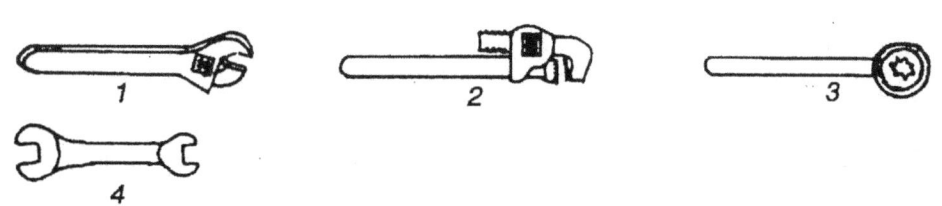

   The wrench that is used principally for pipe work is numbered

   1. 1   2. 2   3. 3   4. 4

3.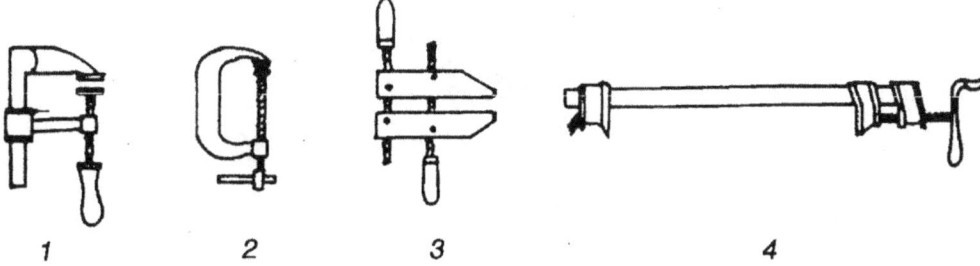

   The carpenter's "hand screw" is numbered

   1. 1   2. 2   3. 3   4. 4

4.

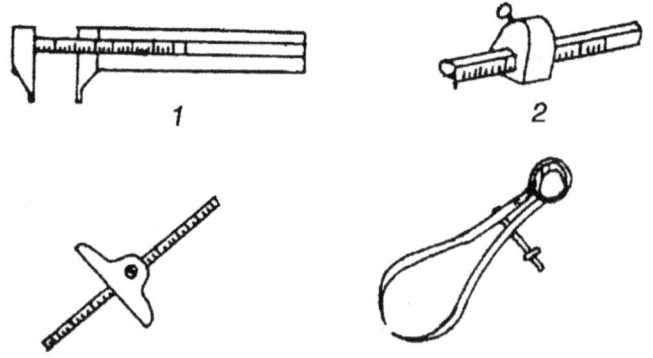

The tool used to measure the depth of a hole is numbered

1. 1   2. 2   3. 3   4. 4

5.

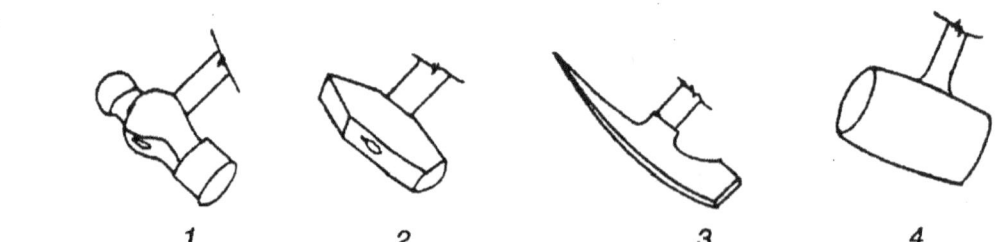

The tool that is best suited for use with a wood chisel is numbered

1. 1   2. 2   3. 3   4. 4

6.

The screw head that would be tightened with an "Allen" wrench is numbered

1. 1   2. 2   3. 3   4. 4

7.

 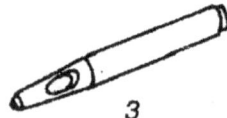

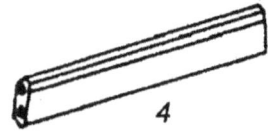

The center punch is numbered

1. 1   2. 2   3. 3   4. 4

8.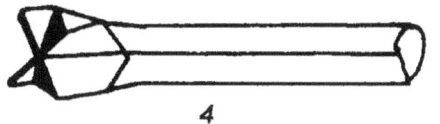

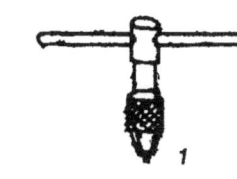 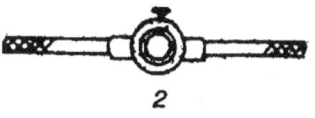

The tool used to drill a hole in concrete is numbered

   1. 1   2. 2   3. 3   4. 4

9.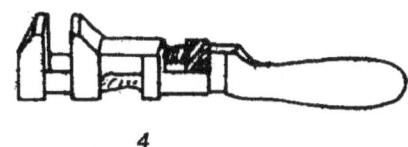

The wrench whose principal purpose is to hold taps for threading is numbered

   1. 1   2. 2   3. 3   4. 4

10.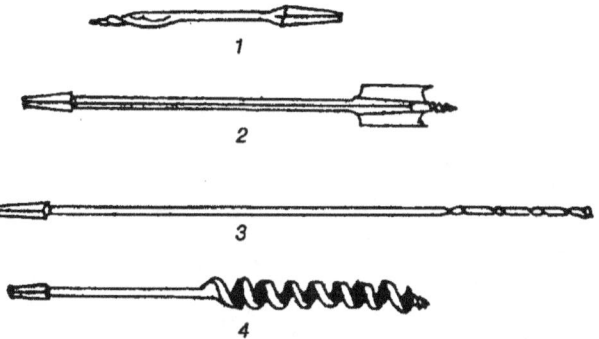

The electrician's bit is indicated by the number

   1. 1   2. 2   3. 3   4. 4

11. The head of a cold chisel is "mushroomed" as shown in the sketch. 11.____
The use of a chisel in this condition is poor practice because
   1. it is impossible to hit the head squarely
   2. the chisel will not cut accurately
   3. chips might fly from the head
   4. the chisel has lost its "temper"

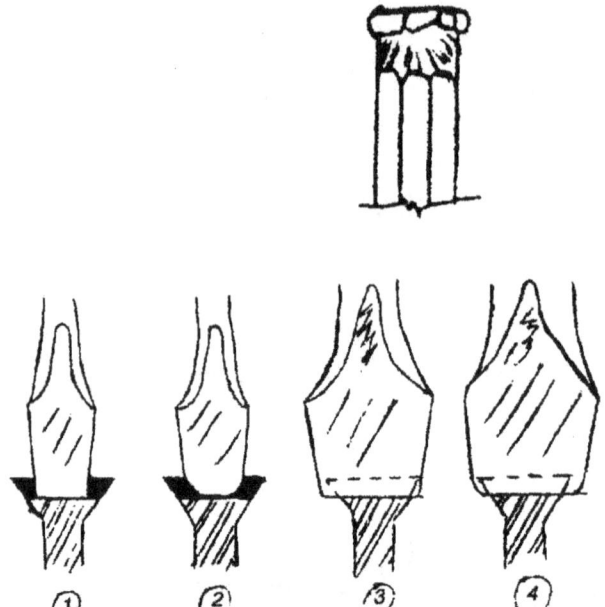

12. The above diagrams show a section of a screw with a screwdriver that is to be used with 12.____
the screw. The one of the diagrams that shows the correct shape of screwdriver is

   1. 1   2. 2   3. 3   4. 4

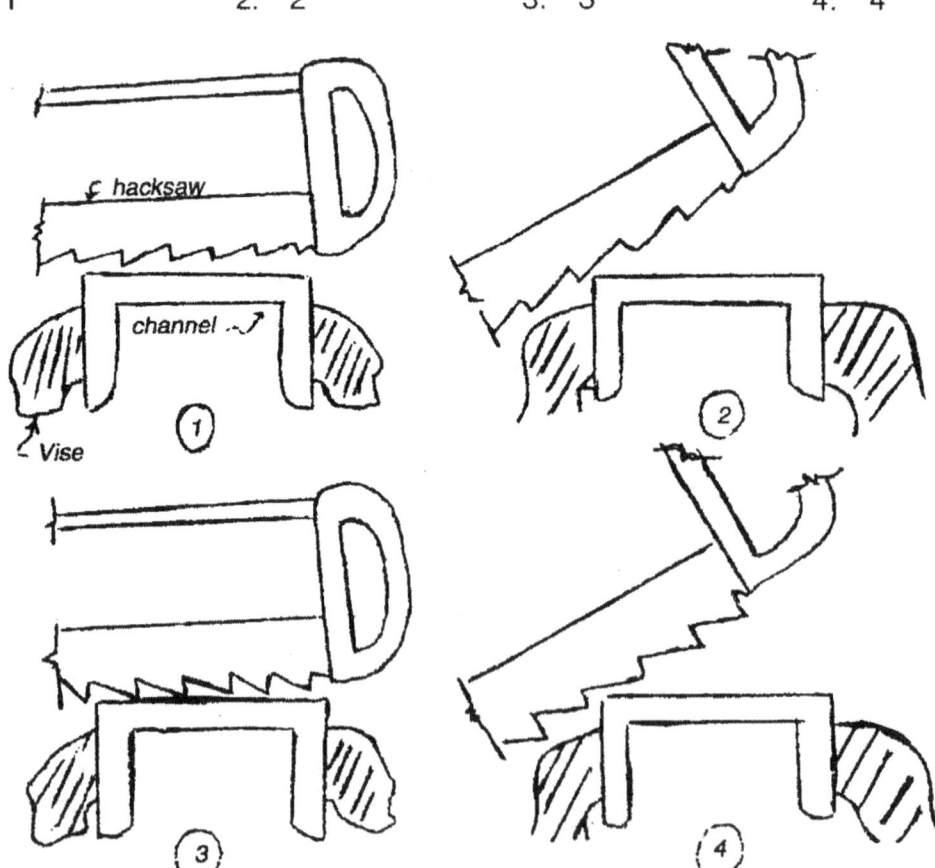

13. A steel channel is to be cut through with a hacksaw. The correct method for doing this is   13._____
    shown in the diagram numbered (diagrams above)
    1. 1   2. 2   3. 3   4. 4

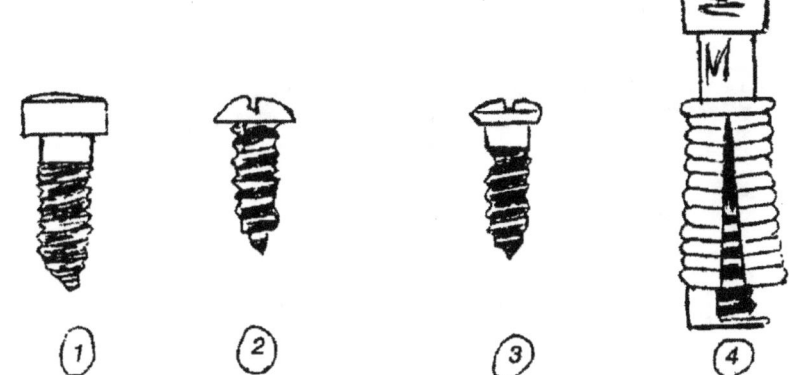

14. The screw above that is most frequently used for sheet metal work is numbered   14._____
    1. 1   2. 2   3. 3   4. 4

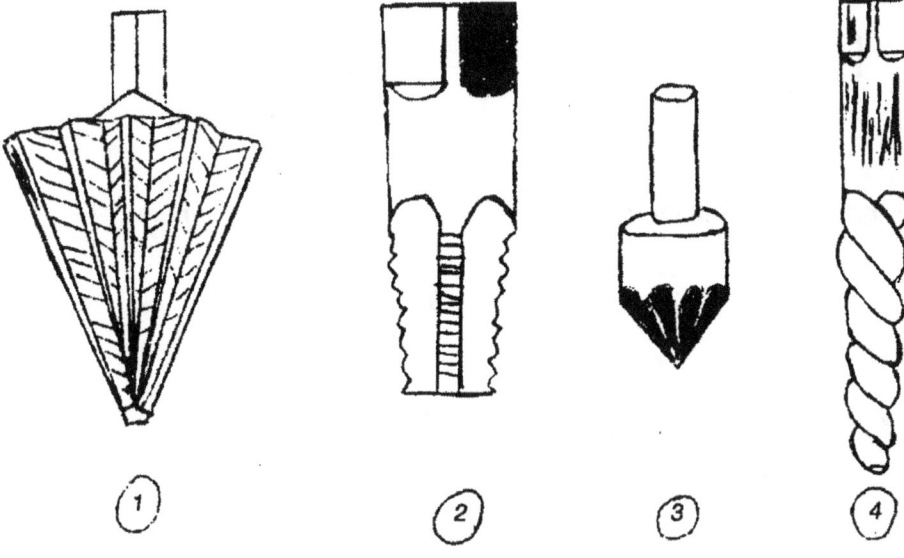

15. The tool used to ream the ends of pipe after the pipe has been cut is shown above in the diagram numbered   15.___

    1. 1   2. 2   3. 3   4. 4

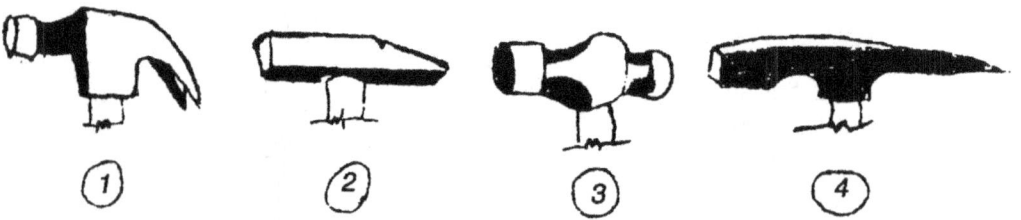

16. The hammer that would be used by a mason to trim brick is shown in the above diagram numbered   16.___

    1. 1   2. 2   3. 3   4. 4

17. The saw intended especially to make accurate miter cuts is shown in the above diagram numbered   17.___

    1. 1   2. 2   3. 3   4. 4

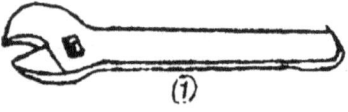 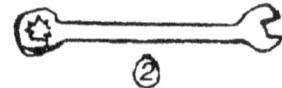

 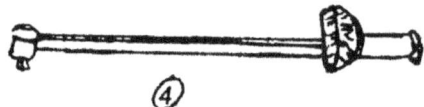

18. A wrench used to tighten cylinder head bolts to a specified torque is shown in the above diagram numbered   18.____

    1. 1   2. 2   3. 3   4. 4

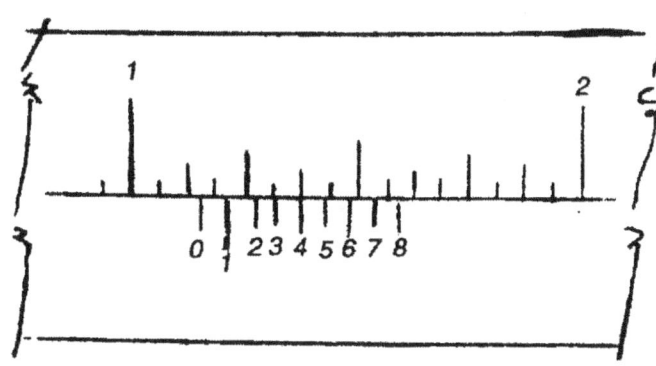

19. A section of the scale of a vernier caliper is shown above. The reading of this caliper setting is most nearly   19.____

    1. 1 3/8   2. 1 5/64   3. 1 5/32   4. 1 7/64

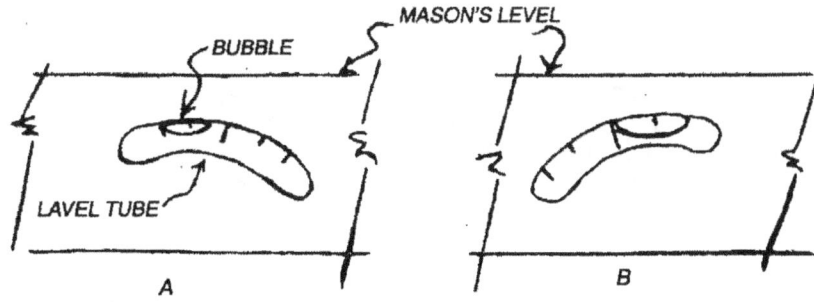

20. A level is placed on a table and the bubble moves to the position indicated in diagram A above. The level is then turned end for end and placed in the same location on the table as before. The bubble now appears as shown in diagram B. The one of the following statements that is correct is   20.____

    1. the left end of the table is higher than the right end
    2. the right end of the table is higher than the left end
    3. it is impossible to tell which end of the table is higher
    4. the level tube is not set properly in the level

21. The flat-head screw is No.   21.____

    1. 1   2. 2   3. 3   4. 4

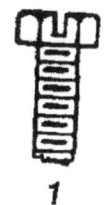 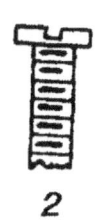  

22. The "Phillips" head is No. 22.___

    1. 1   2. 2   3. 3   4. 4

23. The standard coupling for rigid electrical conduit is 23.___

    1. 1   2. 2   3. 3   4. 4

      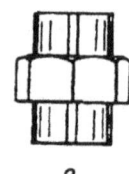 

24. The shape of nut most commonly used on electrical terminals is 24.___

    1. 1   2. 2   3. 3   4. 4

25. The stove bolt is 25.___

    1. 1   2. 2   3. 3   4. 4

KEY (CORRECT ANSWERS)

1.	2	11.	3
2.	2	12.	1
3.	3	13.	1
4.	3	14.	2
5.	4	15.	1
6.	3	16.	4
7.	1	17.	3
8.	4	18.	4
9.	1	19.	3
10.	3	20.	4

21. 3
22. 4
23. 1
24. 2
25. 3

ARITHMETIC OF SEWAGE TREATMENT

The English system of measurements is used for computations at sewage treatment works, except in the case of a few determinations. The metric system will be mentioned where the metric units are used.

Basic Units

Linear	1 inch (in.)	= 2.540 centimeters (cm)
	1 foot (ft.)	= 12 inches (in.)
	1 yard (yd.)	= 3 feet (ft.)
	1 mile	= 5,280 feet
	1 meter (m)	= 39.37 in. = 3.281 ft.
		= 1.094 yd.
	1 meter	= 100 centimeters
Area	1 square foot (sq. ft.)	= 144 square inches (sq. in.)
	1 square yard (sq. yd.)	= 9 sq. ft.
	1 acre	= 43,560 sq. ft.
	1 square mile	= 640 acres
Volume	1 cubic foot	= 1728 cubic inches (cu. in.)
	1 cubic yard	= 27 cu. ft.
	1 cubic foot	= 7.48 gallons
	1 gallon (gal.)	= 231 cu. in.
	1 gallon	= 4 quarts (qt)
	1 gallon	= 3.785 liters(1)
	1 liter	= 1000 milliliters (ml)
Weight	1 pound (lb.)	= 16 ounces = 7000 grains
		= 453.6 grams
	1 ounce	= 28.35 grams (g)
	1 kilogram	= 1000 grams
	1 gram	=1000 milligrams (mg)
	1 cu. ft. water	= 62.4 pounds
	1 gallon water	= 8.33 pounds
	1 liter water	= 1 kilogram
	1 milliliter water	= 1 gram

Definition of Terms

A *ratio* is the indicated division of two pure numbers. As such is indicates the relative magnitude of two quantities. The ratio of 2 to 3 is written 2/3.

A *pure* number is used without reference to any particular thing.

A *concrete* number applies to a particular thing and is the product of a pure number and a physical unit. 5 ft. means 5 times 1 ft. or 5 X (1 ft.).

Rate units are formed when one physical unit is divided by another.

$$\frac{60 \text{ft.}}{2 \text{sec.}} = 30 \frac{(\text{ft.})}{(\text{sec.})}$$

Physical units can be formed by multiplying two or more other physical units.

1 ft. X 1 ft. = 1 ft. X ft. = 1 ft.^{2} (square foot)

Physical units may cancel each other.

$$\frac{6 \text{ ft} \times 7.48 \text{ gallons}}{1 \text{ ft.}} = 6 \times 7.48 \text{ gallons}$$

Per cent means per 100 and is the numerator of a fraction whose denominator is always 100. It may be expressed by the symbol "%". The word *per* refers to a fraction whose numerator precedes *per* and whose denominator follows. Hence "per" means "divided by." It is often indicated by a sloping line as "/."

Problem: What is 15 per cent of 60?

$$60 \times \frac{15}{100} = \frac{900}{100} = 9$$

Problem: One pound of lime is stirred into one gallon of water.

What is the per cent of lime in the slurry?

$$\frac{1}{1+8.33} \times 100 = \frac{100}{1+8.33} = 10.7 \text{ per cent}$$

Formulas

Circumference of a circle $= \Pi D = 2\Pi R$

Area of a circle $= \Pi R^2 = \frac{\Pi D^2}{4}$

$\Pi = 3.1416$
Area of triangle = 1/2 base × altitude
Area of rectangle = base × altitude
Cylindrical area = circumference of base × length
Volume of cylinder = area of base × length
Volume of rectangular tank = area of bottom × depth
Volume of cone = 1/3 × area of base × height
Velocity = distance divided by time. Inches, feet, or miles divided by hours, minutes, or seconds.
  Discharge = volume of flow divided by time.
    Gallons or cubic feet divided by days, hours, minutes, or seconds.
    1 cu. ft. per sec. = 647,000 gallons per day.
    1 mgd = 1.54 cfs = 92.4 cfm

Detention Time. The theoretical time equals the volume of tank divided by the flow per unit time. The flow volume and tank volume must be in the same units.

$$\frac{20{,}000 \text{ gal}}{200 \frac{\text{gal}}{\text{min.}}} = 100 \text{ minutes}$$

Problem: A tank is 60 × 20 × 30 ft. The flow is 5 mgd.

What is the detention time in hours?

1 mgd = 92.4 cfm

$$\frac{60\text{ ft.} \times 20\text{ ft.} \times 30\text{ ft.}}{92.4 \times \frac{5\text{ ft}^3}{\text{min}}} = 78 \text{ min. or 1 hr. and 18 min. or 1.3 hours}$$

Surface Settling Rate:

This means gallons per square foot of tank surface per day.

Problem: If the daily flow is 0.5 mgd and the tank is 50 ft. long and 12 ft. wide, calculate the surface settling rate.

$$\frac{500{,}000 \text{ gal./day}}{50\text{ ft.} \times 12\text{ ft.}} = \frac{833 \text{ gal.}}{\text{ft.}^2 \times \text{day}}$$

Weir Overflow Rate:

This means gallons per day per foot length of weir.

Problem: A circular settling tank is 90 ft. in diameter. The flow is 3.0 mgd. Calculate the weir overflow rate.

$$\frac{3{,}000{,}000 \text{ gal./day}}{\Pi \times 90 \text{ ft.}} = \frac{10{,}600 \text{ gal}}{\text{ft.} \times \text{day}}$$

Rate of Filtration: The mgd is divided by the acres of stone to give

$$\frac{\text{mg}}{\text{acre} \times \text{day}} = \text{mgad}$$

$$\frac{\text{mg}}{\text{acre} \times \text{ft.} \times \text{day}} = \text{mgaftd}$$

An acre-ft. is an acre in area and 1 ft. deep.
A fixed-nozzle filter is 140 x 125 feet. Stone is six feet deep. Flow is 9 mgd. Calculate the rate of dosing or hydraulic loading in mg per acre-foot per day.

$$\frac{140 \times 125}{43560} = \text{acres} = 0.402$$

$$0.402 \times 6 = 2.412 \text{ acre-feet}$$

$$\frac{9}{2.412} = \frac{\text{mg}}{\text{acre} \times \text{ft.} \times \text{day}} = 3.73$$

The BOD of a settling tank effluent is 200 ppm. If 15 lb. of BOD per 1000 ft.^{3} of stone is to be the organic loading, how many cubic feet of stone are necessary with a hydraulic loading of 3 mgd.

$$\frac{200 \times 8.33 \times 3 \times 1000}{15} = 333{,}333 \text{ ft.}^3$$

$$\frac{333,333}{6} = 55,500 \text{ ft.}^2 \text{ for filter area if stone is 6 ft. deep.}$$

Parts per million:

This is a weight ratio. Any unit may be used; pounds per million pounds or milligrams per liter if the liquid has a specific gravity equal to water or very nearly so. 1 liter of water = 1,000,000 milligrams.

   1 ppm = 8.33 lbs. per million gallons
   1 ppm = 1 milligram per liter

A sewage with 600 ppm suspended solids has 600 X 8.33 = 4998 lb. of suspended solids per million gallons.

Efficiency of Removal:

$$\frac{\text{ppm influent - ppm effueny}}{\text{ppm influent}} \cdot 100 = \text{percent efficiency of removal}$$

Percent of Moisture:

$$\frac{\text{wt. of wet sludge - wt. of day sludge}}{\text{wt. of wet sludge}} \cdot 100 = \text{percent moisture}$$

Percent of Dry solids:

$$\frac{\text{wt. of day sludge}}{\text{wt. of wet sludge}} \cdot 100 = \text{parcent day solids}$$

Other calculated quantities that need no special explanation are:
   Square feet of sludge drying bed per capita
   Cubic feet of digestion space per capita
   Cubic feet of sludge produced per day per capita
   Cubic feet of grit per million gallons
   Pounds of sludge per capita per day
   Cubic feet of gas per capita per day
   Kilowatt-hours per million gallons pumped

Specific Gravity: This is the ratio of the density of a substance to the density of water. There is no unit. Density = the weight of unit volume.

$$\text{S.G.} = \frac{(\text{wt. bottle with sludge}) - (\text{wt. of empty bottle})}{(\text{wt. bottle with water}) - (\text{wt. of empty bottle})}$$

1 gallon of water = 8.33 lbs.
1 cu. ft. of water = 62.4 lbs.
These vary slightly with temperature.
   Water at 32° F. = 62.417 lb./ft.^{3}

Water at 62° F. = 62.355 lb./ft.^{3}
Water at 212° F. = 59.7 lb./ft.^{3}
Ice   = 57.5 lb./ft.^{3}

Problem: What is the weight of dry solids in 1000 gallons of 10% sludge whose specific gravity is 1.04?

$$1000 \times 8.33 \times 1.40 \times \frac{10}{100} = 866.3 \text{ lbs.}$$

Mixtures:

If two materials of different percentages are to be mixed to produce an intermediate percentage, it may be done by rectangle method. Problem: We have 30 per cent and 50 per cent material. In what ratio shall they be mixed to produce 37 per cent material.

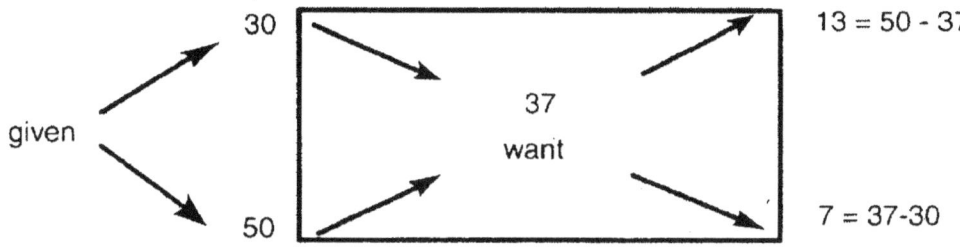

Desired ration is 13 parts of the 30 per cent and 7 parts of the 50 per cent. This will give us 20 parts of 37 per cent.

www.ingramcontent.com/pod-product-compliance
Lightning Source LLC
Chambersburg PA
CBHW082213300426
44117CB00016B/2785